Growing
Where I Was Planted

Autobiography
by Margaret L. Kryder Warren
Founder of Island Poultry Farm, Inc.

Margaret L. Kryder Warren

www.outskirtspress.com/growingwhereiwasplanted

DENVER, COLORADO

Growing Where I Was Planted
Autobiography by Margaret L. Kryder Warren, Founder of Island Poultry Farm, Inc.
All Rights Reserved.
Copyright © 2015 Margaret L. Kryder Warren
v5.0 r1.0

Edited by Judy Le Jeune

Cover Image by Ashley J. Maetozo - used with permission
Back cover author's photograph by Judy Le Jeune
Interior Images by Margaret L. Warren

Outskirts Press, Inc.
http://www.outskirtspress.com

ISBN: 978-1-4787-3453-6

Outskirts Press and the "OP" logo are trademarks belonging to Outskirts Press, Inc.

PRINTED IN THE UNITED STATES OF AMERICA

*This book is dedicated to the memory of my daughter,
Jean Louise Novosel,
with all my love.*

Contents

Acknowledgments

MY SINCERE THANKS to Cynthia Wicker for encouraging me to tell my life story. Your visits and audio-taping our conversations helped keep my story alive for transcription later in the writing process.

My thanks to Laurie Wakefield for her friendship and encouragement throughout the entire book writing experience.

My thanks to Barry Kirk for his technical assistance in preparing the photos for my book and the love and kindness he has always shown me.

My love and admiration to Ashley J. Maetozo for the beautiful young woman she has become and for the inspiration her painting gave me for the title of this book.

My thanks and gratitude to Judy Le Jeune, publisher of *CountyLine* magazine, for her interest in my story, for taking my book jacket photo, for her patience, and for agreeing to edit my manuscript drafts.

My thanks to Jerry Blanchard for his memory of some of the events in this book and for his life-long friendship.

My love to my daughter, Pat Viars, for her persistence and dedication in helping me make my book a reality.

i

My Roots

PEOPLE I HAVE talked with have said that I have had a very interesting life, and many people have said that I should write a book about my life and encouraged me to do so. This book has been years in the making. The following is the whole story. Hang on for the ride!

I will start with my birth on a cold February morning at about four o'clock in the morning, so I was told. It was February 10, 1916. I remember very little of my childhood. I forgot to mention that I was christened Margaret Louise Kryder. I do not know where the Louise came from, but my mother's first name was Margaret. When I was born, I was brought into this world by a mid-wife. It just so happened that my step-grandmother was the person, who was there to take care of my birth. She was a mid-wife and delivered many of the babies in the nearby town of Jersey Shore and the surrounding towns. She is the same woman that was the dominating figure in shaping my mother's life. My mother was 13 months old when her mother died in the great flu epidemic of 1885. My mother was born on March 17, 1884. I never heard much about my mother's first seven years spent with her aunt and uncle, but I know that any love or understanding she learned was in those first seven years. I know this for a fact because I came to know Aunt Becky and Uncle Henry and knew how much they and their children loved my mother and how they grieved when she was reunited with her father when he remarried. From all of the stories that I have been told, those next seven years until she was 14 and went to work in the Woolrich Woolen Mills in Woolrich, Pennsylvania, were the years that made her bitter and not very loving until the day that she died. Her idea of hard work and making money were instilled in me, and I knew no other way of life.

Mother was not able to show affection outwardly, and I think that all of her children missed something in our lives because of that. Her second seven years had a profound influence on her life in her later years. I never remember being held on my mother's lap, nor being told by either of my parents that they loved me.

My mother and father met in 1906 and went together for nine years before getting married. As I understand it, my father was living with his father on the family's farm. My mother said, "I will not marry you with your father owning the farm and us all living in the same house." So my grandfather decided to sell my dad the farm. Since he didn't have any money for the downpayment, my mother gave my father $1,000. She had been working at the Woolrich Woolen Mills for 16 years by then. Being a frugal person, she had saved up money. It is my understanding that the farm sold for around $3,000, which at that time was a lot of money and one of the largest farms in the area.

My mother and father were married on the 17th of March, 1915, which also happened to be my mother's 30th birthday. I guess they lived a blissful life for that year. When my mother became pregnant in May, she would not leave the house after that until I was born. She was embarrassed by being pregnant. When I was about two years old, my mother had a little walker for me and, on a nice day, she put me out in the yard in the walker. I guess I must've been hungry because I started to eat dirt, and it wasn't too long after that until I started passing earthworms. My mother called the doctor right away. When he came in, he said, "I think she ate dirt when she was outside, and she ingested earthworm larvae, and they grew, and now she is passing earthworms." The doctor was mystified because he had seen children with worms, but never earthworms.

My parents were able to make a good living and, in a few years, they were able to pay off the mortgage on the farm. About 1919, when I was three, the old dirt river road from Lock Haven to Jersey Shore, was replaced by the State of Pennsylvania with a new concrete road. The new road went right through the middle of the farm and left us with half of our property on either side of the new road. I decided that I would look out and see what all the new construction and noise from all of the heavy equipment was about. I took off through the field and walked for about a quarter of a mile away from the house. Eventually, my parents missed me. My father had just dug a ditch from the barn into the house to get running water into the house, and the ditch had filled up with water, so naturally the first thing they did was search the ditch for my body. When they didn't find me there, they didn't know what else to do. They had a barn, a chicken house and a pig pen, and they searched these buildings, but not finding me there, my dad decided to go to the construction site. When he got up there, I was watching all of this construction, and my father said to the construction boss, "When you realized that this child did not belong here, why didn't you come to let us know she was here?" The construction boss said, "Well, we thought eventually her parents would miss her and come looking for her." I don't remember whether I was punished for that or not. I think that they were just so glad to get me back that, by the time they found me, they were just happy that I was alive. I was old enough to walk but was probably not old enough to know any better than to do a thing like that.

The second fright was almost a disaster. My father and mother bought a big tractor to take the place of the horses to do many of the chores on the farm. We had what they called "gang plows" and a disc that was hooked on behind the plows. Now, they were able to turn three furrows when plowing the fields instead of one with the horses. Also, the operator was riding instead of holding the plow and walking behind the horses. Disking (pulverizing the ground) was also done in this one operation. My sister was born in June, and it probably was about September when my mother decided to put the baby in a carriage, and we went out to the field to see the new tractor in operation. My dad was driving the tractor, and when we got up fairly close to my dad, he held out his arms for me to come to him. The tractor was still moving. As I ran toward him, I guess I did not know what I was supposed to be doing, so I stopped, but this big machine kept on going, and I was right in the path of the big disc that was still moving. When my dad saw what was happening, he jumped from the tractor while it was still moving and grabbed me just as the machine cut through my little red knee boots that I had gotten the previous Christmas. Because of my dad's quick thinking, I was spared both of my legs. My parents probably got a few gray hairs from that scare. This probably set the tone for the rest of my life because I never feared to tread where other people had not gone. I got myself into some trouble many times over in my lifetime, but I was always able to work things out with little help or advice from anyone.

We did not have many things to keep us entertained back then. We had to make our own entertainment. When I was probably about four years old, I went to our chicken house and got myself some eggs and went out to make a cake in a mud puddle, mixing the mud with the eggs. I knew that there had to be a batter to make a cake because I had watched my mother make a cake before. I knew that it had to be good because it looked like my mother's chocolate cake batter. I don't remember being punished for this, but I guess it was a rather comical thing for a child to be doing. Other than that, I helped my mother weed the garden and entertained myself in this way. We did not have a choice like the children do today, so we were always looking for ways to be entertained.

I have heard that my mother became pregnant again shortly after I was born. Unfortunately, she miscarried that baby. However, in 1919, 18 months after I was born, my first sister was born.

I do not remember the first few years of my life, but after that I started school at the age of 5 ½ years old. That was the same year that my second sister was born and, during that school year, I came down with German measles and brought them home to my sister. That's when we had the big problem with her because she got the measles and nearly died. She was only a couple of months old at that time, and I remember them talking of losing her and how we were under quarantine and had a special nurse come to stay at our house to care for her. Fortunately, she recovered. Mother was also pregnant at that time with her last child, my brother Bud. Heaven only knows how many more children there might have been if that child had been a girl. Needless to say, that child was spoiled rotten and never did recover his whole life. Later in the story, you will understand why I have made this comment.

We called my baby brother, Bud, but his full name was Clarence Filmore Kryder, Jr. When he was four years old, he developed diphtheria, so the doctor gave the entire family toxin-antitoxin shots. Bud and I got abscesses on our bodies from these shots. Bud's abscess developed in his groin, and my abscess developed internally on the sac around my heart. I was in a lot of pain and, eventually, the doctor decided that my abscess should be lanced and drained. He made an incision under my arm, lanced the abscess and packed the wound with long lengths of gauze. Every week he took out about three inches of gauze in an attempt to have the wound heal from the inside out. This was a time when the strawberries were coming in and the health department put a quarantine on our home with yellow tape on the door. We were not allowed to sell any of our produce, so we had to allow people to come and pick their own fruit or vegetables and give us whatever they wanted to pay. The quarantine lasted for three weeks, and we all survived with no long-lasting effects.

We lived out in the country where there weren't any playmates or neighbors close by, so Bud made up a playmate of his own and he called him "Escabob." Bud would crawl up in the maple tree, and he would play with Escabob for hours and hours and hours. Bud had a great imagination. But, at the foot of this maple tree there was poison ivy, so one day Bud showed up at the house with poison ivy. My dad discovered that if you put salt on the poison ivy it would die, so he salted all of the poison ivy he could find near our home.

When I was about seven years old, I was sent to my aunt's for a week of vacation. They lived in a small town about six miles away. On Sundays, we were only allowed to sit on the porch and swing or go for a walk. It was on one of these walks that I started falling down without any apparent reason. My aunt decided that I needed some attention, so she informed my father. Somehow, he got in touch with the Kiwanis of Lock Haven and found out that they had a program where one of their members would pick me up and take me to a doctor, who came to this small town once a month. This doctor said that I had curvature of the spine and flat feet. He decided that I should have my ankles operated on to fix the problem. The day that I went for the operation, I was running a temperature, so he would not operate. He then ordered me arch supports that had to be worn with knee high, lace-up shoes and a back brace of steel and canvas. It kept me straight as a poker and it was very uncomfortable. I had blisters on my hips the entire three years that I wore it. For the rest of my life, until about 20 years ago, my back was poker straight. I guess it was worth all of the misery that I suffered.

My aunts and uncles always came to our house every weekend for dinner because my mother was a wonderful cook, and she never seemed to mind cooking big meals for people. We had a real close relationship for many years with my mother's dad, my dad's two sisters, and my mother's brother and his family. My dad had three sisters, but he only had two sisters living at that time because Aunt Rena had died and left three boys. Two of the boys were grown, but Aunt Rena died in childbirth with her third son, and my dad's mother raised Aunt Rena's son, Linwood. She would also come to the family dinners and, sometimes, she would stay at our home for two or three days with her grandson. She would try to take over the running of our household while she was there, and this caused friction between my mother and her.

My mother, age 2 in 1886,
Margaret E. Getz Kryder.

Emmanuel Getz with his two children.
L to R: Charles, Emmanuel and my mother.

My mother in her early 20s, sitting on the horse having fun with her girlfriends.

Clara E. Kryder
My paternal grandmother.

Aunt Rena's son, Linwood,
and Clara, age 79, in 1940.

On a picnic. Front L to R: Me, cousins Dolly, Francis and Paul Goodman and their mother, Bertha. Back L to R: My dad and Uncle Isaac Goodman.

On a picnic. L to R: Mother and me, Dolly Goodman, Bertha Goodman, Fred Goodman, my father in back, and Paul Goodman next to him.

My mother and father in 1939.

My father and me, age 1.

Me, age 3.

Back L to R: Kathryn and me.
Front L to R: Janice and Bud.

CHAPTER 2

My Birth Home

OUR LARGE FARM was quite removed from any neighbors. Our house was a Victorian style home built in the 1800s. At this time, this home was probably considered an upper class home. There were three porches on the house: one in front leading to the front door, one in back that went to the mud room, and one on the side of the house that went into the kitchen. I have no memory of going in or out of the front door. Inside, the rooms were large, and there were three rooms downstairs and what we would call a mud room the size of a normal living room. The kitchen also served as our dining room. It was heated by a kitchen range that was also used to cook our food. The living room was heated by a tall, round wood-burning stove. It was a rare occasion when we used the living room. Needless to say, we spent most of the winter months in the large kitchen and lingered there as long as we could get away with it because the rest of the house was so cold. Once we were in bed, it was fine because we had plenty of blankets, and we children all shared a room. The room we shared had a hole in the floor above the kitchen that kept it a shade warmer than the other rooms because of the heat rising from the range. They called this heating process "banking it" where they would put in as much wood as the range would hold, allowing for a layer of coal to go on top of the wood. That would slowly smolder throughout the night and, in the morning, the coals were still hot, so they put wood on top of the hot coals for cooking during the day.

There were two stairways that went to the second floor. The stairway that went up out of the kitchen started with two steps that had no railings and led to a small landing. Upon reaching the landing, you made a 90 degree right turn to continue up the remaining stairs that were enclosed by walls on both sides. When you reached the top of this stairway, you came to a hallway. If you turned right, you came to the first door that led into the children's bedroom. If you continued down the hallway past the children's room, you came to our parents' bedroom. If you turned left at the top of the stairway, there was a door leading into a hallway where there were three more separate bedrooms on the left side of the hall. On the right side of the hallway, there was an open railing that wound around to the second set of stairs that I mentioned earlier. When you went past the last bedroom on this hallway, you made a 90 degree right turn into a large room that today we would call a walk-in closet. This room had many shelves in it, and this is what my mother used as a walk-in pantry to store all of the preserves and canned goods that we had prepared throughout the year for the winter months. If you continued a short distance past the walk-in pantry, you came to another door straight ahead at the end of the hallway, where you came into a large room approximately 20 x 30 feet. We kids used it for a playroom in the summer when we were not outside. It was too cold to use in the winter months because it was not heated.

If you went down this second staircase, you came to the front door. This was called the "grand staircase" that you would view if you entered the front door. Coming in the front door, you would also see a hallway running parallel to the staircase that ended with a door that opened onto the side porch.

We children were forbidden to use that side of the house unless we were sent to get items from the pantry. I don't remember why this was forbidden. However, every chance we got, we would sneak into that side of the house and go up to the top of the staircase and slide all the way down the bannister around the curve to the bottom of the railing. It seemed like a lot of fun for us, especially since it was forbidden. I probably was the ring leader in this activity because I was the oldest child.

The mud room was on the back of the house and it had a second range. This was where my mother did the laundry, all of her preserving and canning.

Off of the mud room, there was a "wood house" with a chopping block, where my father chopped all of our firewood and stored it for the winter months.

We did not have indoor plumbing in this house until later on. There was a hand water pump in our kitchen, and it drew water from a well that we had in back of our house. We had to go outdoors through the mud room to get to the "outhouse." The outhouse was about half a block from the house. At night, we had bed chamber pots that were large bowls with handles that we used during the night if we had to go to the bathroom. My mother would carry these down to the outhouse in the morning. When we bathed, Mother brought in a large wash tub and sat it in front of the kitchen stove where she had the oven door open and put heated water in the tub for us to take a bath. We kids all had our baths once a week on Saturday, and we all used the same bath water. As the water got chilled, my mother would add more warm water from the kettle on the stove until we were all bathed.

It is curious that, at that time, we did not have running water in the house unless we pumped it in from the well, but there was running water into our barn for the livestock. I remember this, but I don't know why we did not have running water into the house as well.

When you came out the front door of our house, there was a small porch with three steps down to the lawn that had a large mulberry tree in the middle. My dad made us a swing with a very long rope by tying each end of the rope to a large limb of the tree. This made a large loop, and he notched a board on each end and fitted the board into the loop to make a seat. Many hours were spent pushing each other on that swing. Toward the edge of the lawn grew several lilac bushes, then the lane, the canal, the tow path, the dirt river road, and the banks of the Susquehanna River. When the mulberries were ripe and my mother could not find me, she always looked in the mulberry tree because this was one of my favorite places to be, sitting on a limb as high as I could climb to eat all of the ripe berries I could reach.

The entrance to our farm was off of the River Road. The lane turned right and crossed the canal that separated the two farms that my dad owned. The lane then made a sharp 90 degree left turn and went up by the next two farms, where it then made another 90 degree left and returned to the River Road that continued on to Lock Haven, Pennsylvania in one direction and to Jersey Shore, Pennsylvania in the opposite direction. The only person I remember using the lane was the mailman. Quite often, he managed to get to our house at noon where he would put his horse in the corral to be fed and watered. My mother would invite him to eat many a dinner with us. The farm was bordered on the east by the west branch of the Susquehanna River and the canal with a tow path. That was how lumber was transported very early in the history of Pennsylvania. The logs were made into barges and floated down the rivers and canals and were towed by mules on the tow path.

On our farm, we had a very large barn. It had a ground floor and a second floor that was reached by an embankment at the rear of the barn that was made of stone and earth. Horses could pull the grain, straw and hay from the fields to the barn. The straw was unloaded by a forklift that was pulled by our two horses. The forklift was so big that it would only take two lifts to unload a wagon load of straw or hay. On the left, as you went into the barn, was the straw maw and on the right was the hay maw.

Straw was what remained from the wheat shaft after the thrasher/binder machine went over the field of wheat. The first part of the machine would cut, shell and bag the wheat as it was cut off, and the binder would then cut the remainder of the stem down to the ground, bundle it, tie it off with binder twine, and drop it on the ground. Men would follow this machine and pick up the straw bundles and stack them vertically in the field so they could dry.

When the straw bundles were dry, they were loaded onto a wagon and the binder twine was taken off. The wagon was pulled up the embankment to our barn by our two horses. The horses were unhooked from the wagon and then hooked to the forklift that worked on a pulley system. A pulley on a boom was swung over the straw wagon, and my father lowered a rope with the two forklift arms attached and cradled a large load of straw. Then, he had the horses pull the load up on the pulley, so he could swing the boom arm over to the left side of the barn where the straw maw was formed. We used the straw for bedding material for the horses and cows. My dad and other farmers rented this machine because it was very expensive to buy. During this harvesting period, the surrounding farmers took turns renting this machine, which also included five to six workers. Harvest was a big time for us, and the workers loved to come to our farm because my mother was a good cook, and she always had them for both dinner and supper.

Hay was alfalfa and clover that was used to feed the farm animals. These crops were cut by a mower that was pulled by our two horses. It was left to lie on the ground until it was dried. Before hay balers were invented, the dried hay would be raked into mounds and left to further dry. When it was dried enough to store in the barn, workers would come with pitch forks and throw it onto the wagon, and it was transported and unloaded in the barn just like the straw. The hay was piled in the right side of the barn. Both maws were approximately 20 feet tall. As kids, we used to climb up a ladder near the straw maw and jump in. It was lots of fun. We did not jump in the hay because it could have nettles that could scratch the skin. I remember that our neighbor's barn burned down because they stored hay that was not dried enough. Slowly, smoldering combustion began and turned into a fire that consumed their barn.

In our barn, the straw and hay were placed on the second floor of the barn via the embankment in the rear of the barn. The ground floor was where the animals were kept. The cows and horses each had their own stanchion that was wide enough for them to stand up to eat and lay down. Each animal had its own feeding trough at the end of its stanchion. There was a hole in the ceiling where the hay and straw could be dropped from the second floor and then dispersed by hand to the stalls or troughs.

There was a covered corral in the front of the barn where the animals could roam and a bigger corral in front of the covered corral. The fence to the uncovered corral was also the shared fence to our large home garden.

This garden is where we raised all of our vegetables. On the right side of the garden were four sour cherry trees that kept us supplied with canned cherries all year long. On the left side of the garden, my father planted four peach trees.

There was a path that went between the garden fence and the corn crib, chicken house and smoke house. It was down this path that my father dug the ditch to take the water to the house. After he did that, we had water, but it was always cold. If we wanted hot water, we had to heat it on the stove.

We had pigs, cows, horses, chickens, turkeys, ducks, geese and guineas. The fowl were all free-range. We had a large vegetable garden to keep our family of six well fed for the entire year. The pay crops were wheat, corn, oats, and barley. We killed a steer and seven or eight pigs every year, and we sold what the family did not need. My mother and grandfather would take the buggy and our faithful horse and go into the small town about three miles away to sell our excess food door-to-door. The town folks were always glad to get fresh meat, so selling it was an easy task.

We had one lady, who liked the brains of the pig. My father went to her door and, when the lady's husband answered the door, my dad said, "I brought your wife some brains!" The husband did not know that his wife had ordered brains, so he looked baffled when my father made his announcement. We often laughed about this story at home.

The home where I was born.
This picture was taken in 1914.

The barn on the farm where I was born.
This picture was taken in 1914.

Back L to R: My step-grandmother Emma Getz, my father, my step-grandmother's daughter Aunt Nellie Heppler.

Front L to R: My step-grandmother's grandson Paul Seyler, Aunt Clara, half-sister to my mother, and me. We are sitting on the front steps of my birth home.

My dad (left) on a hunting trip with Bud.
Dad enjoyed hunting and fishing.

CHAPTER **3**

The Fruits of Our Labor

MY DAD AND mother owned our farm, which was 120 acres. My Great Uncle Jeff (my mother's uncle) owned the farm adjoining our farm that was approximately 120 acres. My dad grew vegetables on our farm for our family and for sale to the public. My dad had an arrangement with Uncle Jeff, and he grew wheat, hay, and corn on Uncle Jeff's farm to use as feed for our livestock and sold any surplus. My dad also owned 40 acres of land, about three miles from where we lived, and it was an apple orchard that also had pear, cherry, peach, and plum trees. It had a good many apple trees of different varieties. Every fall, he would hitch a team of horses to a big wagon, and we would go to the orchard to pick the apples. The whole family went on this adventure. My mother would pack a picnic lunch and take all four of us, and we would come home with a full wagon of apples. My father would take the apples to what was then called a "cider press," and he would come home with three barrels of cider. One was to be put in the cellar to make vinegar, and the other one we drank until it had fermented and became an alcoholic drink. I, of course, was never allowed to drink the fermented cider.

The third barrel was made into apple butter. The night before, my aunts would come to our farm, and we would have what they call an apple "snitzing." That meant that you would peel the apples, core them, cut them into quarters, and then place them in big lard cans overnight. That was a two or three day adventure for us children. The adults did all of the work, but the children had a great time because the day and night before was busy with relatives and neighbors coming to help peel and core the apples. My dad's two sisters would come with their children and help prepare the apples for the apple butter. It took five bushels of peeled apples to make about 30 gallons of apple butter.

We used an apple peeler that attached to a bench with a vise-like screw device, and it had a handle on one side and three sharp prongs on the opposite side with a sharp blade that would come down when we turned the handle. The apple was put on the prongs with the small end of the apple toward the prongs. When we turned the handle, the blade would come down close enough to just touch the apple and peel continuously around the apple in a spiral until the apple was peeled from top to bottom. An assembly line of people was formed, and the peeled apple was passed to the next person in line, who cut the apple in half. The next person would take out the core. The next person would cut the apple into fourths. We had quite an assembly line going, and I think this may have been where I learned about the efficiency of an assembly line, which I later used successfully in my business. The apples were put in big lard cans until about three the next morning when my father would get up and build a big fire under the 50 gallon copper-lined kettle that was on trestles in the front yard. He would put a barrel of cider made from the apples from our orchard and watch for it to boil. While the cider was heating and condensing down, we would do our chores like milking the cows, feeding the stock and feeding the chickens. When it condensed down to about half the amount originally put in the kettle, Dad would start to put in the apples. Someone had to continuously stir the apples with a long handled wooden paddle for hours. This was a slow and hard process, and it would be evening until the spices were added to the mixture and cooked a while longer. Then, the kettle was slowly emptied into gallon crocks and sealed with paraffin so that it would not spoil. The balance of the apple butter was put in quart jars and canned so that we could sell them in the little market that we had by the roadside in front of our farm. Sometimes, my mother would help with the apple preparations if she was not busy making a good meal for everyone to eat. The adults were glad for this day to be over, but the children could not wait for the next bread baking day, so we could have hot bread and the newly made apple butter. Still one of my favorites! It was really a special treat if Mother had just made cottage cheese to eat along with the bread and apple butter.

To make cottage cheese, she would take a gallon crock of fresh milk from our cows and set it on the side of the stove, for about a day, until the milk had soured. She would then pour the soured milk into a cheese cloth bag and hang it on the clothesline to let the curds separate from the whey, which took a couple of hours. The whey dripped out of the bag and, when the curds were dry, she would put them through a potato masher and then mix them with good rich cream.

We would put the cottage cheese on the hot bread and top it off with apple butter. Yum! Since we had milk cows and, therefore, had our own fresh milk, we often had ice cream as a treat. It was made with good heavy cream, and we were never short of fresh whipping cream for the many pies and puddings that Mother made.

Back then, we did not have refrigerators or freezers. We did not even have an icebox. In the winter, my dad and a neighbor would go down to the Susquehanna River and chop out blocks of 12 inch thick ice and bring it home on the wagon. Our neighbor had a large sawdust pile on his farm that was about eight feet tall and as big as a large room. They would bury the ice blocks under the sawdust, and it would insulate the ice blocks all summer long. We only used the ice for making ice cream. When Mother wanted to keep other food cold, she would take it down to the cellar that had a dirt floor and was cool in the summer.

One of our favorite meals to this day, even one of my great grandchildren's favorite, is "pot pie." It is not what most people think of when you say pot pie. My mother would take a quart of her homemade canned pork sausage and brown it in a big kettle and then add water, celery, onions, and some carrot slices to make a good rich broth stock. She would bring this to a boil and, while this broth was cooking, she would make pie dough and roll it out thinly on a floured board and cut the dough into three inch squares. She also peeled two large potatoes and diced them. When the broth came to a boil, she would start adding the dough and potatoes in layers, stirring it often to keep the dough from sticking together. She would then put on the lid and slowly cook it for 20 minutes or until the potatoes were soft. We called it "pot pie" because it was pie dough cooked in a pot. The only ingredient that I changed over the years was to use fresh chicken broth stock and pulled chicken because I was in the chicken business.

One of the other favorite meals was pork and sauerkraut with mashed potatoes and homemade apple sauce. Our heritage is German, so this was a meal we enjoyed, and all of my family still enjoys it today. My mother would put a loin of pork in a large roaster and put it in the oven for about one hour. Then, she would add her homemade sauerkraut all around the pork loin. This would slow cook for several hours. About 15 minutes before the meal was ready to be served, she would make a dumpling and drop it by the tablespoonful on the sauerkraut.

My mother made sauerkraut in the fall when the cabbage was picked to prepare it for the winter months. We would make 10 or 15 gallons of sauerkraut by shredding cabbage and putting it in a five or ten gallon crock in layers with salt in between the layers. Each layer would be stomped with a wooden mallet until we could see juice, or brine as it was called, before adding another layer. When the crock was full, we would put a dinner plate over the opening and put a well-washed stone on top of the dinner plate to hold the cabbage under the brine. We could hardly wait for a dinner of pork and sauerkraut. To this day, it is still my most favorite meal.

Today, we get about four country-style pork ribs and put them in a crockpot for one hour on high. Then, we turn the crockpot down to low and put in two medium sized cans of "Silver Floss" sauerkraut and let it all cook for about six hours. Near the end of the cooking time, we may throw in some hot dogs that are also good with sauerkraut. Silver Floss brand sauerkraut is the closest one to tasting like my mother's homemade sauerkraut because it is crock-cured like homemade sauerkraut.

Another interesting thing we did in crocks was to stand cucumber pickles on end in rows around the crock and, between each layer, we put washed grape leaves and dill from our garden. It was also covered with salt brine and weighted down with a dinner plate and a washed stone. This was another "cannot wait to eat goodie."

Before it was time for the chickens to stop laying eggs in the fall, we would preserve a few crocks of eggs for cooking and scrambling. This process was done by standing the eggs on end, lining a crock until it was full, and covering it with a solution made from a product called "Water Glass" that my father bought at the store. They were carefully weighted down and kept for later use.

In the summer, we were all kept busy storing food for the cold winter months. My mother liked to have six to eight hundred quart jars of meat, vegetables and canned fruit to feed our family, as well as food for the hired help and the many relatives and friends who came calling on weekends. We always had at least 100 quarts of tomatoes and another 100 quarts total of green and yellow beans, yellow and white sweet corn, peas, lima beans, carrots, beets, sweet pickles, pickle relish, bread and butter pickles, ketchup, peaches, pears, red sour cherries, and plums. We also had jars of jellies and jams made of strawberries, blueberries, red raspberries, rhubarb, currants, peaches, pears, and blackberries.

Since we raised most of our food, it was either fresh or canned from our garden. No pesticides were used. We used to get potato bugs and my dad would pay us one penny for every hundred potato bugs that we would pick off of the potato vines. As we picked them off the plants, we put them in jars so my father could dispose of them later. This assured us a good potato crop.

My father worked in this same little town on the railroad. They had shops where they built the railroad cars. He walked to and from work and would bring the few items we needed from the grocer that we could not produce on our farm. The items we had to buy were: coffee, tea, sugar, oatmeal, cornstarch, baking soda, baking powder, coconut for pies and cakes, salt, pepper, and spices. At Christmas time, we got nuts in the shell, a little candy, and an orange for each of us.

Things were simple in those days, and it did not take much to make us happy.

CHAPTER 4

My Early School Days

MY SCHOOL DAYS were spent in a one room building accommodating eight grades. In the winter, it was heated by a pot belly stove, and it was cooled in the early fall and late spring by having the windows open. The windows were also the only source of lighting. On a dark, dreary winter day it was helpful to have good eyes. The stove was fueled by wood, and I never did know where or how that wood got there, but there was always a big pile of it there when we came in the mornings. The most important part of my education in those early years was not to ever be late for school or to miss a day and to get 100 on the spelling bee every day. At the end of the term, we received a certificate for having 100% attendance and never being late.

One cold and frosty morning, the windows of our house were all coated with frost and there was close to three feet of snow on the ground. I was dressed and ready for school since I could not miss a day. My father brought the big gray horse from the barn, and my mother took me out on the porch and handed me up to my dad on the horse. He took me to school, and the snow was so deep that his feet drug in the snow all the way to the school. I guess that was the first that I had really noticed the wood by the stove because I was taken into the school house, and my boots were removed, and my dad rubbed my feet and hands to get them warm. Shortly, the teacher came, and my dad got on his horse and went home. When school was out, my dad was there again to give me a ride home. I must mention the bathrooms. Behind the school building, about 30 feet away, there was one little building for the girls on the right side and one on the left side for the boys. If you had to relieve yourself during school hours, you raised your hand with one or two fingers, depending on what kind of relief you needed. I never did think about why it was important for the teacher to know that, but now as I think on it, maybe it was the length of time it would take to do each task.

Needless to say, one year I missed the spelling bee because I misspelled the word Pittsburgh. I forgot the "h" and my father was so disturbed about this that he went to school the next day with me to overturn that ruling. However, I never have forgotten the "h" again. Life went on for several years, and I went to a new consolidated school in 8th grade and, needless to say, it was a struggle for all of us coming from this backward one room school. I was in 5th grade before my dad discovered that we were not being taught any English. Upon further investigation, he discovered that the school did not have any English books. The teachers never told anyone that they had no books. So you see, we had our "slackers" back then also. It all did not happen in the generations to follow.

Me, second from the left in the front row, sitting on the steps of our school with all the students, grades 1 through 8.

CHAPTER 5

Bobsled Hayride

IT WAS SOME time in the years before we moved to the new house that I had the great experience of going on a bobsled hayride. We had a large team of horses and a bobsled that was nothing more than a big, long box with sled runners. It was probably as wide as our modern-day, large-size car and two times as long. The horses wore the most beautiful sounding set of sleigh bells and, as they trotted along with their load of young folks and my family as chaperones, we would sing all kinds of songs. The best one, of course, was "Jingle Bells." My dad hired out to some groups, but the Sunday School classes he took for free. The sled bed would be full of straw, and my mother would heat bricks and bring many warm blankets to keep the merry group warm. It was seven miles to my grandmother's house on my paternal side and we would go there, and she would have hot chocolate for the young people and, of course, coffee for the grownups. We would start about dusk and return home sometime late that night.

CHAPTER 6

Elder Blow Wine

WHEN I WAS six years old, my father made what he called "elder blow" wine that was made from the flowers of the elderberry bush. It was supposed to be for medicinal purposes only. Every time we got a sniffle or running nose, my mother would give us a tablespoon of the wine soaked in brown sugar and that seemed to do the trick. We never had colds as youngsters. I am sure that we did not use all of the wine by the end of the winter; however, the wine was always gone by spring. I am beginning to think that maybe my dad needed a lot of medicinal reasons for the use of that wine. Although I never knew my dad to drink, I wonder what did happen to that wine? All that I know is that it cured whatever ailed us, and we never needed to call a doctor. My mother would make a pie from the elderberries when they were ripe. She did not do this often, but I remember a few times. The only other time that I remember my dad touching alcohol was when the Junior Chamber of Commerce had a luau in my backyard in the 1970s. My son-in-law was a member of the Chamber of Commerce and asked if the Chamber could hold their event on my property. They dug a pit and filled it with stones and built a fire. When the rocks were hot, they filled the hole with potatoes, corn and oysters. After several hours, they uncovered the hole and had a feast in my backyard under the canopy of a large weeping willow tree. A young man put a keg of beer under the tree and, sometime during the evening, I saw my father coming out from under the tree. I said, "What were you doing under there?" and he replied, "I just had a sip of that beer. I never tasted it before, and I wanted to see what it tasted like." That is the only time that I know of my dad tasting alcohol. He did not smoke either, so I do not know of him having any bad habits. I know that he was a good man, and he certainly was a good father.

CHAPTER 7

Great Depression Aftermath

THIS WAS ALSO the time when our great country was still feeling the effects of the Great Depression, and many people came rapping on our door for handouts or some were asking to work. Wages then were 50 cents a day and room and board. We were very fortunate to have a black man come to our door, and my father decided to give him a chance to work. His name was Charlie Brown. We never did find out if that was his real name or not, but that is what we called him. We gave him blankets, and he slept on the hay mound in the barn. He was a great black man, and we children became very fond of him. When my mother came down with the "sick headache" as she called it (we call them migraines today), it was that time of the month, and she would be so deathly sick that even a slight noise made her throw up. Charlie Brown would come in and cook for us. One of the things he made that I still remember and like was canned salmon with sweet onions sliced on top and covered with vinegar. Makes my mouth water just thinking about how good that tasted. He was with us for several years, but he never would sit down at the table with us to eat no matter how many times we asked him. It was a sad morning when he did not appear for his breakfast. He just disappeared, and we never did hear from him again.

Charlie was the first of many men my father hired from the traveling beggars. I remember one man, and I do not remember his name, but he wore a wool hat all summer long in the heat of July and August. My mother often wondered why the hat. Well, come September when we started to school, we found out. By that time, the head lice had found their way to our little heads. One evening, we were sent home with a note telling my parents that we could not return to school until we had no more lice. It seems that we had carried them to many of our classmates. Mother was so embarrassed, but my grandmother said she would fix that problem before we had to go back to school on Monday. The treatment was harsh, but the results were good. She washed our heads in kerosene twice a day, and we were back in school on Monday. That was my one and only experience with head lice.

It was a few years after we moved in 1932 or 1933 that I remember people still coming to our door for food and shelter. With some of the people, we really feared for our lives, although we always let them stay in the barn and handed them out a warm meal. They were usually gone by morning.

CHAPTER 8

The "Homestead"

IN 1926, MY father decided to build a new home on the other side of the new highway, which ran through our farm. He started to build it and, as he ran out of lumber or needed more, he just started tearing down the house where we were living. It went room after room until the only room left was our kitchen. He had a good-sized garage built at the new site, and we went there at night to sleep as he tore down our old home for lumber. Finally, there was nothing left of the old house but the mud room and the room above it. We had to move to the new big garage. There was only one man building the new house, so we had to live in the large, two room garage for three years until the new house was livable. The garage consisted of one large room upstairs where all of our dressers were lined up on one wall and all of our beds were lined up on the opposite wall. Today, this would look somewhat like a military barracks. The large room downstairs was our kitchen, dining room and living room. All the rest of our furniture was placed around in this room.

We had a range for cooking and no electricity. The outhouse was about half a block away across a small bridge that straddled a small trickling stream that ran behind the garage.

At night we had chamber pots under the beds in case we had to go to the bathroom in the night. In the morning, it was my mother's job to empty the chamber pots.

Three years later, when we finally moved into our new house, we took all of the old furniture with us, but it did not come close to filling this large home. This new house would have been a beautiful home if it had ever been landscaped properly on the outside or finished off properly on the inside.

The inside was made of solid black walnut in the foyer staircase, living room and den, and the dining room with solid oak. The kitchen was done in pine with cupboards along one side with a sink in the middle. On the other side, there was a large table and the range was on the end of the kitchen facing the outside door. It was a large eat-in kitchen. In this new home, we had one powder room off the kitchen and a full bathroom upstairs. This was the first time we had indoor plumbing and that was quite a luxury for us.

Mother never took much interest in the house as far as decorating it, furnishing it or cleaning it. I never have been able to figure out why. I think she just had too many other daily chores to do plus taking care of a husband and four children. She also made a lot of meals for relatives and guests, who were welcome at our home anytime and dropped in frequently. By this time, I was in 7th grade, so it became my chore to clean whatever was cleaned in the house.

My father never mowed the grass or pulled weeds, and they were about 24 inches tall. I would get out the old push mower and try to mow it.

We have always referred to this home as "the big house," and my parents lived in this house until 1960, and it is still a beautiful house today. The people who currently own the home were very kind and generous to allow me to visit my childhood home in 2012. They told us that when people ask them where they live, they say the home on Kryder Hollow and people still say, "Oh, you live in the 'big house.'" They have maintained it beautifully to this day.

Since we had a large farm, we had plenty of fruits, vegetables, nuts, apple butter, etc. to take care of our needs, so Dad put up a little building by the highway, and it was my job to take care of the customers at the roadside market. The customers would come out from town, pull up and, if I was not right there, they would blow their horn and I would come running. It did not matter if it was in the middle of a meal or not. That was my job until we closed it when I was in 10th grade. My mother spent all of her time in the fields making sure that we had plenty of things to sell. She would go and pick wild blackberries and blueberries to sell also. We sold everything in the market that we raised on our farm, and we raised a good many crops of fruits and vegetables.

In early spring, my mother would grind horseradish, and we would sell it in jars. A funny story can be told about my mother and the grinder. She thought that she might be able to use the grinder to grind coconut instead of scrapping her knuckles on the grating board when trying to make coconut for our cakes and pies, which we all loved. She ground the coconut and, when we tasted it, guess what it tasted like? Horseradish! You see the grinder was meant to be used for grinding horseradish.

And of course, the fall before, we had made 100 gallons of apple butter, so we had it put in jars and sold it in the spring. We had black walnut trees and, during the winter, for our entertainment, my dad would crack the nuts, and we would pick out the goodies and sell them in the spring at our little roadside stand. When I came home from school, my dad would bring in about a peck of navy beans that had been harvested and put them on the table. It was our job to sort the beans from the stones and other debris. We would be rewarded after we sorted the peck of beans and did our school work by playing dominoes for a while, until it was time to go to bed. This was our daily routine until the bean crop was all sorted and ready for sale.

We always had a very big breakfast because we always had hired hands to help with the crops, and Mother had to feed them a good breakfast. So, she would have fried potatoes, pancakes, eggs, and either bacon, ham or sausage, and coffee. Breakfast was always our biggest meal of the day. For that reason, we never had any trouble getting help on the farm because they liked to come to our farm to work and to eat, and the going pay was a dollar a day. These workers were local neighbors, who needed work and did not have farms of their own. They plowed our fields and planted crops like corn, wheat, oats, barley, and tobacco. These crops where the larger money-earning crops. The wheat and corn were also the crops that we would take to the grist mill to grind into flour and cornmeal that we used to feed our own family.

Every fall, we slaughtered a steer and canned the meat for our own use during the winter. We also slaughtered seven to eight pigs in the fall and made pork loin, bacon, sausage, ham, cracklings, lard, scrapple, and liverwurst. We took our horse and buggy to the next town filled with these products and sold them door-to-door. What we did not sell, my mother preserved for our family to eat over the winter.

The other items we sold at the stand were lettuce and onions, since they were the early crop of vegetables that came in first. The next crops we had to sell were the peas and then all of the other crops were sold as they were harvested: radishes, beets, cabbage, rhubarb, corn, cucumbers, cantaloupes, watermelon, strawberries, red and black berries, and currents.

My father used a part of our yard that was at the side of our new house as a flower field. He would scatter poppy seeds and then plant sweet peas. When they blossomed, I would make a bouquet of sweet peas and poppies and some baby's breath to decorate the counter of the stand. The people that came to buy from us were the wealthy people from the nearby town of Lock Haven. They were the ones that owned the theaters, the brick plant, the leather company, the paper company, and the chemical company. They all had their chauffeurs and the passengers sat behind a glass divider, so the passengers had some privacy from the driver. The women would be smoking a cigarette, using their long cigarette holders. They would always hold them down when they came to the stand, thinking that no one could tell that they were smoking cigarettes. I could see the smoke coming up above the car window, so I knew what was going on. But anyway, one day a lady came by and bought the bouquet of flowers that I had made. She took them home, and the next day they came and the chauffeur handed me a dollar bill. When I asked him what the dollar was for, the lady in the back seat said that when she got them home and put them in her vase, they were so beautiful that she just had to come back and give me another dollar. So, from that time on, I figured I was pretty good at making bouquets, so I always kept a bouquet on the stand, just in case it would sell.

I had to be out there all the time. Since I was the oldest child, it was expected that I would take on the roadside stand responsibilities. I was so little that my dad made a box for me to stand on, so I could see out the stand opening and serve the customers who stopped to buy produce.

I remember that my mother taught me how to make change by practicing with me. She would pretend that she was a customer and she bought 80 cents worth of groceries and gave me a $20.00 bill. I started with 80 cents and counted out change until I got to $20.00. I was naturally good with numbers, so making change came easily for me. I will always remember the black money box that I had, and it opened up on leather hinges. I remember one night, when I sat down at the foot of my mother and father's bed and counted the money I had taken in for the day, I had over $100. I remember it as clearly as if it was today. I said to my dad, "If I had made only 19 more cents today, I would've had enough to pay your insurance premium for a year." A hundred dollars back then was a lot of money.

The stand was not very fancy and was made rather crudely. The stand had windows on both ends, and the front opened up by a pulley on a rope that we tied to a hook on the inside of the small shed. Before electricity came through our area, we would hang kerosene lanterns on the corners of the shed and keep open until the car traffic stopped passing the stand. At the end of the day, we untied the rope and lowered the window and called it a day. I never thought of this task as a hardship because I liked talking with people and making money. This probably was the motivation of my life to work for myself and also make a living.

I found out later in life that I was not very good at working for other people because I could always see a better and more efficient way to do things than were being done by others. As my own boss, I could run the show like I felt was most effective. I think I was born with extraordinary common sense that cannot be taught or learned in school. I honed this skill from an early age at the roadside stand.

I knew how to handle money, make money and count money by the time I was 8 ½ years old. People would come and say to my mother that they could not believe that this young girl was changing $20.00 bills. I am not sure exactly when this happened, maybe around nine or ten years old, but it was when I was still very young that I decided that my goal in life was to become a millionaire.

My mother's goal in life was to make money. Housework never interested her. She and my dad would go to the mountains and pick 50 quarts of wild blueberries to sell at the stand by the side of the highway. They took a "wash boiler," which was what we heated water in to wash our clothes and take our baths. It was filled to the top with blueberries, and they also had buckets filled with blackberries.

I remember one time when I was about seven, and they were off picking blueberries, and I was watching my little sister. I decided to try and bake a blueberry pie. My sister was three years younger than I was, and she was just old enough to get into everything. We were still living in the temporary garage, and the flour was in the bottom shelf of the cupboard in our makeshift kitchen. I was working away on the pie and, when I turned around and looked to see what my sister was doing, she had gotten in the flour and had it all over the floor. Not only did I have to finish the pie, but I had to clean up all of the flour before my parents came home. My mother was not very happy that I attempted to make a pie in her absence, but she did give in and say that the pie turned out quite well and was tasty. After that, I was a very good pie baker, until I had a small outlet store and started buying Sexton brand pies, and I figured that they could make them a lot better than I did with a lot less trouble, so I quit baking pies. My daughter, Jean, said, "Mom, I can't understand why you don't bake pies anymore because yours were always so good and now all you do is get the pre-made pies from the store and bake them."

One day, one of the patrons, who regularly came to the roadside stand, pulled into our driveway. They handed my mother a doll and said, "This doll is for your little girl." I remember thinking that it must be for me because they did not know my little sister. My first doll. I never had a doll until that time. I was excited to think that it would be given to me. To my dismay and disappointment, my mother gave the doll to my little sister.

When I was in my 80s, my dear friends Debra and Chad O'Brien, came to visit me in Florida. They knew I was a big Penn State fan and they brought me a present. When I opened it, I found a Penn State Barbie Doll. I looked at Chad and told him that this was the first doll I had ever been given. What a delightful surprise. My first doll!

The "Homestead" home. This picture was taken in 2013.

CHAPTER 9

Church

MY FAMILY WENT to the Charlton Methodist Church from the time I was little. When I was about five years old, my mother got angry about something that happened at church, so she quit going to church. I never did know what happened to anger her. My father taught the Men's Sunday School class, and he took all of his children to church every Sunday. When I was about 15 years old, the church needed a Sunday School teacher for the children. I volunteered and taught for about three years. When a child had a birthday that week, I would make cupcakes and take them to church. The birthday child got a candle on his or her cupcake. I was given a pamphlet with the appropriate Bible verse that related to the sermon for that day. I tried to relate that verse to their everyday lives that was age appropriate. The age range was about four years old to eight years old.

CHAPTER **10**

My First Boyfriend

IT WOULD NOT be a good story without a bit of romance. Our family friends, from Williamsport, Pennsylvania and their sons would stop by our house to visit, and Mother would say as she saw them drive in, "Go down to the cellar quick, and bring me up a couple jars of meat and some vegetables." Meantime, she would be putting together the ingredients for a crumb cake for dessert. When the meal was over, it was my job to clear everything away and do the dishes. Their oldest son always helped me with this chore. This continued for a few years and then one Sunday they came again and, after dinner, my father suggested that we go for a walk to check on the crops growing on the other farm. Back then, that was our entertainment. After about a half mile of the walk, with the six of our family and the four of them, Paul said, "Let's run and hide from the other kids." I do not know if the young man had anything in mind or not, but when his mother missed us, she came storming up and immediately took her family home. My mother did not seem to be upset, or at least she did not say anything about the incident. I was about 15 years old at the time. They never did come back after that, until one Easter a number of years later, and by that time I was married and had my little girl, Jean.

One day, after my husband went to work, I drove to my parents' home. Sure enough, the same family drove into our driveway. The same meal was served and, as always, Paul and I were to take care of the dishes while the younger children and our parents visited. While we were doing the dishes, Paul looked at me and said, "I wish we could turn back the pages of time." That was the last time I saw him and the first time that I was aware that he had feelings for me. I often wonder what my life would have been like if we had been allowed to go together. His mother had said once that their coming to our house was always at Paul's suggestion. Even to this day, I have dreams of this young man. To me, he is always young. We will never know how that romance could have ended, and I will never know if he was as naïve and innocent as I was or not. I have heard that he has since married, and I hope that he has had a wonderful life.

CHAPTER 11

Higher Education

I FINISHED MY 8th grade education and started high school in Lock Haven and went by public bus transportation seven miles each way for the next four years. My parents insisted that I take the academic program, which included Latin and French, two of the subjects that I was doomed to fail because of not having any background in English. I struggled through the courses because I was supposed to be preparing for college. After getting started on that path, college was never mentioned again. So, I was without any preparation to earn my way once I graduated from high school.

Well, about the early part of my senior year, I met a man seven years my senior. He had a car and what was considered a good job at that time. He came regularly to call, and I became quite fond of him. He seemed to have plenty of money and a car, which easily impressed a young girl, who felt lucky to be courted by such a gentleman. He was always a gentleman, although he told me of some of his affairs with other girls, and I began to wonder why he treated me with such respect, but he did.

It was about this time that we had a home economics teacher that I later realized was way ahead of her time in sex education. She taught me how to make Eggs Benedict and that was fine, but when she handed out a book called *Sane Sex Life and Sane Sex Living*, it went around the class and, when it was my turn to take it home and read, I realized that it was something that my parents would not allow me to read. I locked myself in my bedroom and proceeded to read the book. Well, when my mother found out, the roof just about came off the house. So, in a huff, I called my gentleman friend, and we took off for Cumberland, Maryland to get married. Little did I know that I was jumping out of the frying pan into the fire. When I came back, my mother disowned me and never did get over it until five and a half years later when he and I divorced.

My high school graduation picture.

CHAPTER **12**

My First Marriage

WE WERE MARRIED in Cumberland, Maryland because there we did not have to wait three days for a marriage license. We came back home and lived with his parents for about two weeks. I did not like that situation, so I decided to look for an apartment. I found a nice little, brand new apartment with three rooms: a kitchen, living room, bedroom, and bath. It also had a sun porch and was a second floor apartment. We went to the furniture store and bought enough furniture to make the house quite livable. We furnished the living room, kitchen and bedroom for $750.00. Of course, we had to buy this on the installment plan, which was a very little amount per month. When my husband got his pay check of $30.00 every other Friday, he would bring it to me, and I managed the budget. I had to take out $15.00 per month for the rent. Then, I would make a menu for two weeks and then a list of all of the groceries we would need for that week's menu. I would always put a dime in the corner of the cupboard in case we needed to buy a pound of hamburger or a gallon of gas. I would list the other debts we had and make sure that they were all covered for the month. In the fall, when I got pregnant, I would add the cost of flannel to make baby clothes and even put down the nickel it cost for a spool of thread. My husband always wanted me to make sure I budgeted for cigarettes and gasoline. I had the budget down to the last penny.

Life went along fairly well until I went to get the groceries at the store recommended by my husband, and he told me just to put it on his bill. The man behind the counter looked at me and said, "I cannot put this on the bill. He already owes too much and is not making any effort to pay it." Well, that was a shock because he had been living with his parents before we got married. I could not see why he would have a big grocery bill accumulated before we got married, since he had lived with his parents. I'm not exactly sure how I did get the groceries, but somehow I managed it. That was the first shock I had. The second shock came that following fall when he took the wheels off of our car and put them in the walk-in closet in our apartment. I did not understand this, but he said it was because the roads were always bad and that he did not drive on them. It seemed a little strange to me because even his parents and everyone else was driving their cars. For that winter, I had to buy a little red wagon and pull it to the grocery store every payday and buy enough groceries until the next payday in two weeks. When spring came, he put the wheels back on the car, and I thought that we were all set to go. One day, I was at the living room window, and I saw the car going down the alley, and he was in the kitchen. I went to the kitchen and said, "Somebody stole our car and is taking it down the alley." He replied, "Oh, that could be because I still owe $29.00 on the car." The car was being repossessed! I went to my father and asked him to help me get the car back. We had to go to the courthouse, and the car was being auctioned off on the courthouse steps. My dad paid the $29.00, plus costs, and we now had a car again.

After we got our car back, my husband decided he would teach me to drive. The car was a black 1929 Ford Coupe with a rumble seat. Of course, cars back then needed to be cranked with a removable handle in the front that was below the front bumper and attached to the starter for the engine. It was very hard to crank and sometimes it would "backfire." If you did not know enough to let go of the handle quickly, the handle would forcefully start turning backwards and could throw you to the ground. I had seen this actually happen to my husband on several occasions when he was starting the car, so I knew to be cautious when cranking the car. Also, there was no such thing as an "automatic gear shift," so shifting gears also had to be mastered in order to drive the car. When the car was already started and all I had to do was drive it, I learned how to use the clutch to shift gears, and I did it fairly well, without too much jerking. One peculiarity that this car had was that it would not pull up any kind of steep grade in the road. I would have to turn the car around backwards to take it up any hill of significant slope. There were not that many cars on the road back then, so backing up the hills did not seem to be a traffic problem. I don't think this problem was inherent in the make and model of the car, but it was just our particular car. Maybe we would call it a "lemon" in today's world.

Many weekends in the summer, we would pack a picnic lunch, and my girlfriend and her husband would crawl into the rumble seat, and off we'd go for a fun day at a park.

One day, there was a knock at the door. When I answered, it was a man from the clothing store collecting for a suit that my husband had bought. He said it had been over a year, and he had not made a payment. This made me very angry, and I was not very nice to the man. It was not his fault that my husband had not made payments. I informed him that I would pay for the suit, but I did not have the money at that time. He left in a hurry down the stairs. I never heard anything more from him again until I went in to pay the bill, which was six or seven months later, after I had saved up the money from my husband's paychecks.

It was sometime during that summer that my baby brother, Bud, who was about nine years old, came to visit us. My husband liked Limburger cheese and it smelled horrible, but it did have a good taste. When we sat down to the table, my brother said, "I'm not going to eat any of that stuff." My husband told him that it would grow hair on his chest. After taking a couple of bites, he looked up and said, "How much of this stuff do I have to eat to get hair on my chest?" Of course, my husband began to laugh because he thought it was quite a joke.

Anyway, among the other things that I had for dinner that day were mashed potatoes. Since I did not have a potato masher, I had to mash them with the bottom of a glass. My brother went home and told my mother that she should get me a potato ricer for Christmas because my potatoes were lumpy. That's how I got a potato masher.

Things went along quite a while without incident until October when I became pregnant with my first child. I was sick for a few months after that, but I never said too much about it. One Sunday afternoon, we were supposed to go to my husband's parents' home. I was feeling bad that day, and I said, "Let me eat a few soda crackers and lay down for a few minutes. Maybe I'll feel better and feel like going." He grabbed me by the sleeve of the jumpsuit that I was wearing and ripped the sleeve off the jumpsuit. He said, "You're not going to lie down, and we are going to go right now." That was the very beginning of the rest of my life with that man. He could use any excuse to beat on me. One day, he came home from work and started beating on me. I found out that it was because his sister-in-law supposedly told him that I was going to go to my parents' home to have the baby. I was making baby clothes and storing them in a cedar chest at the foot of our bed, and I tried to convince him that I was preparing to go to the hospital to have the baby. I think it was just another excuse to beat on me. That was just one of the many times that I took a beating because of something that his family had told him or supposedly told him.

After the baby was born, his mother began telling him that the baby should be baptized in the Catholic Church, so every time he stopped on his way home from work to see his parents, he came home and beat me. I don't see why I had to come up in conversation whenever he stopped to see his parents. When my daughter was one year old, I decided that it did not matter to me as long as she was baptized a Christian, so to keep peace in the family, I said OK to baptizing her as a Catholic. Since I was not a Catholic, I had to have her baptized in the foyer of the Catholic Church because I was not allowed to go in the church. Since I never knew of him to attend church one time when we were married, I took my daughter to my church every Sunday. My minister asked me if she had ever been baptized, and I told him that she had been baptized in the foyer of the Catholic Church. He suggested that I have her baptized on Easter in his church, since she and I went there all of the time anyway. That way, she would have her membership letter at the church she attended. As it turned out, my husband had to work on Easter Sunday, so I did not tell him about the baptism. Somehow, he found out and took her Easter basket and threw it up against the wall, making a large hole in the plasterboard of our apartment. Of course, life was miserable for a few days after that. Now, my daughter was baptized twice. Maybe that was why she turned out to be such a good girl. She attended this church her whole life and brought her three children up in this church also. She gave me three beautiful grandchildren, so I cannot have any remorse for what I had to go through to raise that child to maturity.

After the first year, my husband found excuses to beat on me. While we lived in our first apartment, the first year we were married, I had a warrant sworn out for his arrest after four beatings. I always dropped the charges when he said he would never beat me again.

It was not a really easy life for me because to do the laundry, I had to get down on my knees and scrub it on the washboard in the bathtub. When I got all the clothes washed, I drained the tub and filled it back up with rinse water. Then, I had to ring them out by hand and take them downstairs to the clothesline to hang them to dry. I continued washing this way until after the baby was born, and I saw an ad in the newspaper that one of the furniture stores was having a sale on wringer washing machines for $29.95 and, along with that, you got a chest of silverware with your initials on it for free. Many years later, I sold that chest of Oneida silverware to an antique dealer in Florida for $75.00.

When I got married, in 1934, my sister decided that she would get married also. She was sixteen years old. Since she did not have any place to live, she persuaded me to look for a bigger house that would accommodate both families. I looked around and found a place that had a full downstairs and an upstairs with four bedrooms. Two of the bedrooms were separated by a bathroom and steps and then there was a third bedroom that I used for a nursery. We turned the fourth bedroom into a nice living room and bedroom for my sister and her husband, and they took their meals with us. This worked out for about three months when, one day, she came home and said that she had found an apartment. That left me with a much larger house than I needed and also a much larger rent payment. This worked fine for them until she became pregnant and she was sick most of the time, and her husband was not making enough money to take care of her and the other expenses. So, they decided that they would move in with my mother and father. They lived with my mother and father until she was about five months pregnant and, one day, her husband did not return home from work. He had walked out on them, and this left her in a position of having a baby and no way to take care of it.

Around this time, my father and mother were having their farm sectioned off into lots with the idea of making a development. Back then, there were not as many regulations as now, so it was just a matter of having a surveyor come in and map it out and have it recorded at the county seat. My parents decided that each one of the four children should have a lot, so being the oldest and the one most settled, I got the first lot.

On March 17, 1936, we had a big flood on the Susquehanna River and lots and lots of things floated away from Lock Haven and other places in its path. Fortunately, for me, a lot of lumber was left deposited on the banks of our farm. Since I was planning on building a house on my lot eventually, my dad suggested that my brother, who was 14 years old, take the big old flatbed wagon that was pulled by one of our horses and go down and load up some of the drift lumber. So, we took off on our mission without a thought of danger. All went fine with the loading, and we started for home. My brother wanted to drive, so I let him, and I was sitting on top of the lumber. There was a house that we had to pass and they had a big dog. It came out and barked at us, scaring the horse and, when he bolted, I flew off and fell under the wheel of the wagon. Needless to say, there was no way for me to keep from being run over. The wheel caught me on my right side, just below my rib cage, and crossed and came out on the left side right below my rib cage. I guess that it was fortunate that when I fell, it was on my face. When my husband came home, my parents insisted that he take me to the hospital for x-rays. It turned out that nothing was broken. As I remember back, I do not recall even being very sore.

In 1937, my sisters and brother and I had the good fortune to come into an inheritance from my mother's Uncle Jeff, who was never married. He split his assets into 33 shares. His nephews and nieces each got two shares, and his great-nephews and great-nieces each got one share. My share was about $2,000.00, which was a lot of money in those days. I put mine in the bank with the idea that someday it would help us to build our own home. My mother used her two shares to buy Uncle Jeff's farm when it went up for sale. This now gave my mother and father the ownership of two farms, which my dad continued to farm until he retired.

After my sister's baby was born, she had inherited the same amount of money as I had inherited, so she decided to go to beauty school. No one in the family, except me, knew how to drive, so I drove her and another friend to Harrisburg to take their final test to be licensed as beauticians. My sister was fretting all the way to Harrisburg that she feared that she would not pass the test. Her friend kept reassuring her that she would pass. As it turned out, my sister passed the test the first time and her friend, who was not worried about the test, did not pass.

There was nobody to take care of her baby, so I decided that it would be a good idea for me to move in with my mother and father, which served two purposes. I could take care of her baby while she went to school and save my rent money to add to my inheritance to build a new home on the property that my father had given me. By then, my sister had graduated from beauty school and was ready to start out on her own. She heard of a shop that was for sale in Wellsboro, Pennsylvania.

The beauty shop was in a large front room of the apartment, and the rest of the apartment was living area. I kept her baby for about three years until her beauty business was established, and then she took the baby with her. She was a good beautician and did very well from the very beginning. She met a young man there and, after about a year, she was married again and soon became pregnant. She kept on working until the baby was born. She was married for about a year and a half and she again was divorced. She still had her good business and was able to take care of the two children. One day, she called me to ask for my help cleaning up after a fire. I dropped what I was doing and immediately drove 80 miles to help her.

During all of this time, I was working to take care of my own child. Sometime later, she called and said that she had found another house, with the beauty shop on one side of the house with living quarters of a kitchen, dining room and living room on the first floor and three bedrooms and a bath on the second floor. It was a really nice house, but she did not know how to go about getting a mortgage to buy it. I put on my one good outfit and my fur coat and went up to her bank. They did not want to give her a mortgage, but I told them that I would co-sign. After I told them I would co-sign, they gave her the mortgage, and I never did have to co-sign. I really could not afford to co-sign anything, but I guess my appearance gave them the impression that I was prosperous. She was only there a couple of years until she again called to tell me that she had another fire and would I come and help her clean up the mess? She seemed to get along very well and looked very prosperous when she came to visit me. She would come almost every Sunday and bring her children for a meal. It was always interesting to see what new outfit she would be wearing that day. She had a couple of fur coats and many Castleberry knit suits.

Throughout my life, each time a sibling called me to come and help them, I would drop what I was doing and go to them and do whatever I needed to do. In my entire life, not one of my siblings ever came to help me. I never asked them to and I never expected them to help me. I was the oldest child, and I was the "go to" person. Even in the 1972 flood, when my home and business were devastated, not one of them called me or offered to help me.

In 1939, I started checking with different contractors and different house plans and finally decided on a plan and a contractor. The total price was $3,750, and I already had almost $2,000, so I am feeling pretty lucky. When it came time to sign the contract to build, my husband signed his name and I signed "Louise K. Wise" and this made him really mad because the "K" stood for my maiden name, Kryder. It was a New England style house with a nice foyer, living room, dining room, kitchen, large laundry, full basement, a fruit cellar, powder room, three large bedrooms, hardwood floors, hot air furnace, and a brick fireplace.

Then, the trouble really began because my mother insisted that the lot and the house on the lot be put in my name only, and so it was. I do not know if it was because she could see trouble coming or if it was because she had such a dislike of my husband, but my mother did not want to put my husband's name on the deed to the lot. I was glad for the gift and built the house according to plans, and it seemed to be with my husband's blessing.

However, soon after we moved in, he became quite violent every time he came in from work and insisted that the house be put in his name. I was tempted different times, but some sixth sense held me off. The beatings continued even after we had left our rented apartment in town and came to live with my parents to save money. He would come in from work in a rage and just start beating on me. My mother and dad were working when these beatings would occur, so they never knew about them.

My husband and I had been in our new house for about a year when my father had gotten a permit to kill deer, out of season, in his apple orchard. The deer would eat apples from the trees as high as they could reach. We used the apples for a source of food for the family, and he also wanted to use the deer meat as a source of meat for his family. He did not want to kill these deer for sport. This permit was granted because money was scarce after the Great Depression, and he wanted to support his family. So, he was granted permission to kill deer on his property out of season. My father had been permanently disabled since he was a young man in an accident on the farm, so he could not haul in a deer by himself. When he asked my husband to help him, he said, "No, I am not going to do anything illegal." We tried to convince him that it was not illegal, but he would not help. Somehow my father got the deer and had somebody else bring it in.

One evening, my husband was working the 3-11 shift, and I took my daughter and went to my parents' home to have dinner. He had forbidden me to go to my parents' home. The next morning, my daughter, in her innocence, said to him, "Mother and I went to Grandma's last night and had a good venison dinner." Then he looked at me and said, "Why would you do that when you know I like venison?" That was when he said that he was going to shoot my daughter and me. He started upstairs where he kept his hunting rifles. That was it for me. I took my five-year-old daughter, my knitting bag and all the clothes that I could carry and went to my parents' house. Our house was about five lots away from my parents' home and, at that time, there was only one house between my house and their house. It was open fields. I quickly decided to take the public highway to their house because I was afraid that he could get a better shot at us with his rifle if we took the alley. When we reached my parents' home, my mother said, "Why are you bringing all of your things over here?" And I said, "Well, I guess I'm moving in." This was kind of a shock to my mother, although she did say that she could see that I was not content. Of course, she did not know why. I had never told them the life that I was living because I felt that it was my fault. I never returned to that house again. He lived in that house for about four weeks and kept coming to my parents' home to see me, but I would never see him. One day, I did see him, and he coaxed me to come back and said that he would never abuse me again. By that time, enough was enough, and I had moved on mentally. He was not an alcoholic, just a mean man. We know today that this is the classic "battered wife syndrome," but back then, the woman always thought it was something she was doing wrong to elicit this kind of abuse from a husband and that she could somehow make it better. I continued to stay with my parents and was finally able to rent out my house that I had built.

We were divorced shortly after this time, and he paid me $7.50 a month for child care. Pearl Harbor was attacked, and he was drafted into the Army when war was declared by Franklin D. Roosevelt. After he went into the Army, I started getting $32.50 per month from the U.S. Government. After he went into the service, we did not hear from him anymore. He never did mistreat our little daughter, but she was old enough to know what was going on by the time we broke up.

The first home I built, in 1939, with my inheritance from Great Uncle Jeff.

CHAPTER 13

My First Job

IT WAS HARD for a while to get a job to support myself and my daughter, but after many interviews, I was hired at the stocking factory in Jersey Shore, Pennsylvania. The pay structure was 25 cents an hour or per piece, whichever was more money. This was when there were seams up the back of the silk stockings before they were made of nylon. It was my job to sew the flat stockings up the middle of the back. I would sew a little way, and then I did something that made me skip a space and this happened all of the way up the stocking. It did not take me long to figure out that I was not cut out for this work.

I had friends who lived in Elmira, New York, and they persuaded me to go to Elmira with my little girl to live with them while I pursued work. The only job that I could find was a job sewing diaper bags for babies. My job was to sew one of the seams on the diaper bag. There was someone standing over my shoulder all of the work day, urging me to go faster and to make more pieces. I observed how they treated the other employees, and I stayed for a couple of weeks until Pearl Harbor was attacked by the Japanese in December 1941.

My parents took me in, and I finally was able to rent the house I had built and that gave me a little income. I was fortunate to be hired for training with Sylvania Electric.

In 1942, there was an ad in the paper that they wanted people to take a test to go to work for Sylvania. You had to pass the test to be considered for a job. We had to go to Emporium, Pennsylvania, which was about 80 miles from home, and it was a cold February day. We went on a bus and, when we stepped off the bus, we were in nine inches of snow. After going to the hotel and finding out that there were no rooms available, they referred us to a home that did temporary boarding. We were able to rent a room for several weeks. After about two weeks, we were able to find a permanent room to rent. We had to take all of our meals at a restaurant. At that time, everything was very cheap. It had to be cheap because our starting pay was 41½ cents per hour and even that seemed like big money. We got a Union and then my wages went up to 48½ cents per hour. I was really making big money and could dress rather well because you could get a nice blouse with matching turban for a dollar. Shoes and all other apparel were priced accordingly.

I took my daughter, who was in first grade, on Sunday evening to a lady by the name of Mrs. Haight, who took care of her during the week while I was away at work. I picked her up on Friday night on my way home. My mother had to go back to work at the Woolrich Woolen Mills because my father had been hurt in a farming accident, so she could not take care of my daughter during the week.

We were in Emporium for about three months when they had a flash flood. The water came down the street like a river. The plant was right in the path of the storm. We were being prepared to work at a Sylvania plant being built in Montoursville, Pennsylvania, which was about 40 miles from where I lived. There were several people working at the plant from our area. A couple of us were able to get a ride with one of these people, who had a car and worked at that plant. His car was an old dilapidated car that had a leak on the passenger side. It was OK on a dry day, but we got a little wet if it rained. We rode with him for six months when we were given a raise in pay. It was not much of a raise. On the way home, the driver told us that he was raising the price for riding with him. It was about the amount of the pay increase that we had just received and that did not sit well with me. I said, "Stop the car because I am getting out." I took the next bus home. By that time I had an old car of my own, so I was able to take the other passenger with me, so his ride fare hike backfired on him!

I wanted to buy my small daughter a wool coat since I was making a little bit of money. I picked one out at a department store in Williamsport, and I had to put it on lay-a-way. I didn't know how I was going to pay for it, but I was determined to get it for her.

They had a pool at work every week, and you would put in $.50 or $1.00 (I can't remember which), and if they pulled your name, you got the money in the pool. I did not play every week because I did not have enough money to waste. However, that one week I did play, and I won $25.00. That was how I bought her new wool coat. It seemed that a "way" was always provided in some manner in my life, just when I needed it.

My first car when I worked at Sylvania.

CHAPTER 14

My First Daughter, Jean

MY DAUGHTER WAS such a good baby, and she seemed healthy, except for getting an ear infection in the winter time every year. Her first ear infection was when she was only eight months old. These infections continued every winter and became chronic.

After my divorce from her father, in 1940, when she was five years old, she developed an ear infection that would not respond to conventional treatment. I finally took her to an ENT doctor in Williamsport, Pennsylvania, and he performed a mastoid operation on her ear, but it was not a successful operation. This did not stop the ear infections or earaches, and they kept getting worse and worse. This doctor had done all that he could do and referred me to an ENT doctor in Bellefonte, Pennsylvania, who was involved in a trial of sulfa drugs, which were experimental at that time. I had to monitor her every 20 minutes, day and night, looking for a reaction of any kind. She had no reactions, but her condition kept getting worse.

The doctor suggested that I take her to a city hospital either in Philadelphia or Baltimore. He had connections at Temple and also at Johns Hopkins. The head of the ENT services at Johns Hopkins was his roommate in medical school. I made arrangements to take her to see him. I took her on the train to Baltimore. He agreed to take her case and perform an operation. It was a very special operation because none of the doctors had ever seen a case like this, and they considered this a very rare medical condition. He gladly took on the challenge since it was a rare case.

I was fortunate to have a cousin living in Baltimore, who was gracious enough to let me stay with them. Jean was scheduled for the operation, and my cousin and I went to sit in the waiting room to await the outcome. After about four hours, she said that she had to go home to fix dinner for her husband, so now I was alone. Each time I saw a gurney go by with a sheet pulled up over the body, I was so afraid that it was my baby on that gurney. I ran out only to be told that it was not my baby. Interns came out to give me updates every few hours, but now I was getting the feeling that things had not gone well and that they were not telling me. It was almost five hours when they came and told me that I could see her back in her room. Her head was all bandaged, and she did not look like my little five year old.

I stayed with my cousin at night but went to the hospital every day. After the first week, the doctor said, "Mother, I know that you are having a hard time financially, and I think you should go back home and go to work." He said that they had a fight on their hands. Each day when I left the hospital, it took them a while to calm her down. The doctor felt it would be better if I left her in their care, so she would not get so upset when I left her each day. He said, "I will call you every day to update you on the progress she is making." That was one of the worst days of my life, when I had to leave my darling baby daughter there. She was not supposed to know that I had gone back home, and they kept her very busy during the day to keep her occupied. Later, I found out that the nurses loved her and treated her very special.

The nurses told me that they had a special area for sick children in the hospital, where they went to play every day. Jean would go there every day to play with the children and would act like she was the mother of the children, bossing them around. The nurses also let her carry sheets to the laundry chute, when they were changing beds, so she thought she was helping them.

The doctor called me at the end of the two weeks and said that I could come and pick up my daughter. When I went to pick her up, she was walking down the hall with a sheet in her arms. I told her it was time to go home, and she said she couldn't go home with me because she needed to stay and help the nurses. She really was not a baby anymore but in first grade. She would always be my baby, no matter how old she became. She was so busy pushing sheets down the chute to the laundry that she did not want to leave. She said, "Mama, you went home." I said, "How do you know that I went home?" She said, "All the kids from my first grade class wrote me a little note telling me that my mom was there to tell them that I was in the hospital and would not be back to school for a while."

I had started to gather money, knowing that I would need to pay the medical bills since my insurance was not in effect yet, so my employer was very gracious and guaranteed me $500 against my future earnings. I asked my father if he would sign a note at the bank for $1,500, thinking that this was not going to be enough to cover the expenses, but at least it would tide me over until I could make enough money to pay whatever the cost was going to be.

Before my daughter and I left the hospital, we were taken to the doctor's office, and I was beside myself with worry because I felt sure that I did not have the necessary funds to pay the bills. I asked how much I owed, and the doctor got a kind of grin on his face, and he said, "I will have to think about this. She did bite me when I examined her, and then I had to grease the wheels on the gurney every time they wheeled her up here because she said they were too squeaky." By now I know that I will be a lifetime paying all of these expenses. He began to laugh and said, "Would five dollars be too much?" I was without words and am not sure that I ever did thank him properly. I just broke down and cried. After a long silence on his part, he said, "I do not want you to pay the hospital bills because I have talked to Blue Cross/Blue Shield and explained the circumstances. They said that all of their money for their region had not been used up and, maybe, they would be able to pick up part of the hospital bill." As it ended up, I paid only $29.00 for the hospital bill. God was surely sitting on my shoulder that day!

I saw the local doctor in Williamsport after I brought her home from Baltimore. The doctor at Johns Hopkins wanted her to have radiation treatments after the surgery as a further precaution. These could be administered in a town near our home in Williamsport, Pennsylvania. I took her to the doctor's office on my way to work. After her treatment, I would pin a note to her coat with my mother's address where she was to be dropped off, and put her on the bus to go back to my mother's home. I went on to work from there.

My baby was well, although her left inner ear was completely gone, leaving her deaf in her left ear for the rest of her life. But, she was back home and healthy. The local doctor said that it was a miracle the way the operation turned out, but it was disappointing for me because she never had any hearing in her left ear.

She was smart and did very well in school and graduated with her RN degree and was a wonderful nurse. I was always so proud of her. I often wondered if her chosen vocation was influenced by her early experience in Johns Hopkins Hospital and the wonderful nurses and doctors who cared for her.

In 1957, Jean graduated from nursing school, and she and her fiancé, Richard, were getting married. They had a beautiful wedding. Richard invited a couple of friends from Idaho to the wedding. They had been shipmates when he was in the Navy. The first couple of nights that they were in Pennsylvania, they stayed at Richard's home, which was 35 miles from where I lived. Richard gave them instructions to get to the wedding. On the day of the wedding, when they started out, instead of going east, they turned and went west. After about 50 miles, they decided that they were going the wrong way. They turned around and came back and got to the wedding in time for the reception. After that, they came to my house and stayed for two weeks. I thought I was never going to get rid of these boys. It turned out that they did not have money enough to go home. We got in contact with their parents, and they wired them enough money to get them back to Idaho. Thinking back on it now, it is a funny story. I don't know what ever happened to these lads, but I never heard from them again.

Jean wanted to start a family right away. Every month after that, she would come tearfully to me and say, "Mom, I am not pregnant." After about eight months, she came one day and joyfully told me that she was pregnant. She and her husband raised a wonderful family and saw that they all graduated from college. She nursed and took on second jobs that she could do from home in order to be with her children as they grew up.

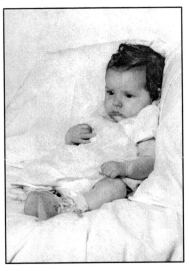

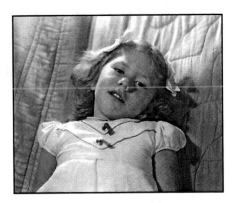

Jean, 4 months old.

Jean, 5 years old.

Jean, age 20.

Jean, age 22, and her future husband, Rich, in 1957.

Jean's wedding photo in 1957.

Jean and Rich in the 1980s.

CHAPTER 15

My Grandchildren

MY DAUGHTER'S PREGNANCY went well. Her doctor was delivering babies using hypnosis techniques on the mothers for an easier delivery with natural childbirth. She had prenatal training with him practicing this technique. When they called me on November 27, 1958, which happened to fall on Thanksgiving Day, I went to the hospital as quickly as possible and waited with her husband for the birth of their first child. We sat for two hours, waiting for them to come out and tell us that her child was born. Instead of that, all of a sudden, she came through the swinging doors with her baby in her arms. She did not seem like she had gone through childbirth and was beaming over her new baby.

Her first child was a boy, my only grandson, and he got his degree from Penn State and is now a comptroller for a large well-known company. His first marriage ended when his wife sadly died from a long battle with cancer. They had just adopted a little boy, the "light of their life" when her cancer came back a year later, and she did not survive. My grandson was shaken to his very core. Now, he was alone, working and trying to raise a toddler. He found a wonderful woman to be his wife, and she was willing to take on the challenge of raising a small boy and considers him her own son. They also have two other boys together. They have a wonderful family, and my grandson is a wonderful father to all of the boys. He and his wife stay very active in the boys' lives with sports and whatever else the boys are interested in experiencing. They live in Delaware.

My daughter's second child was a girl, born 18 months after her first child. When people would see me, they would ask, "Did Jean have her baby yet?" I would say, "Didn't I tell you that she will not have her baby until July 29th, which is her birthday?" Sure enough, she had her second child on the morning of July 29th. She had the hypnosis method with this birth also. By the time I got to the hospital, the birth was over, and my daughter went in the wheelchair down to the nursery to show us the new baby.

This granddaughter graduated from Pitt University and went on to medical school in Philadelphia and now has her own OB/GYN practice in Florida. She married and had two children, a girl and a boy. When I lived in Florida near her, many of my friends went to her practice, and they would always tell me what a delightful granddaughter I had and how satisfied they were with her medical services. She resides in St. Augustine, Florida.

My daughter's third child was a girl. Six years after she had her second child, they went to Olin Mills to have a family portrait taken because they felt their family was complete. Before they got the finished proofs, my daughter discovered that she was pregnant with her third child. It was a shock when they first found out, but after the news sank in, everyone was delighted and anxious for the baby's arrival. She has been such a blessing to her whole family.

She graduated from Indiana State University and has a Master's degree in Occupational and Physical Therapy. She has also been successful in her career and is married and has two boys. She and her husband are also very involved with their boys' activities in all kinds of sports and other interests.

My grandchildren and great-grandchildren have given me much joy, and I love each of them with all of my heart.

Easter 1974. L to R: Grandson Greg, me, Jean, Granddaughter Sherri, Rich, and Granddaughter Tami in front.

Greg and family in 2014. L to R: Great-grandson Gregory Richard, Grandson Gregory Scott, Melanie, Great-grandson Caleb, Great-grandson Brandon.

Sherri and family in 2014. L to R: Great-grandddaughter Ashley Jean, Granddaughter Sherri, Great-grandson Sean.

Tami and family in 2013. L to R: Barry, Great-grandson Kyle, Great-grandson Ryan, Granddaughter Tami.

CHAPTER 16

My Second Marriage

I CONTINUED TO work at Sylvania, and my daughter and I lived with my parents until 1944.

My brother went in the service in January 1942, much to everyone's relief. By now, he was so out of hand that he was driving my parents crazy. He would come in at night drunk and abusive. He was a good looking lad, and the girls went crazy after him, and he was getting all of the favors and bragged about it as well. He was quite a rounder. My parents tried locking him out, but he would break in and have my parents up the rest of the night. He did boot camp and then his tour in the European theater. He then was based in Wyoming. The brother-in-law of the one nice young lady he had dated was also stationed there. She was infatuated with my brother, so she went on an extended visit with her sister to be near my brother.

In 1943, my brother came home on furlough from the Air Force, and he brought his buddy home with him. His buddy flew on the same plane with my brother during World War II when they were flying missions over Germany. My brother was a navigator, and his buddy was a gunner.

His buddy was very nice looking, charming and fun to be around. We dated all the while he was home with my brother. After their furlough was over and they went back to their base in Pueblo, Colorado, he kept corresponding with me. We corresponded for about six months, and he asked me to come out to visit in Colorado for a week. My brother came home on furlough again, this time to get married, and he talked me into going back with him. I took leave from my job and went for a month. I took the train from Jersey Shore, Pennsylvania to Pueblo, Colorado. I stayed with my brother and his wife, who lived in a trailer near the base.

I came back home and we continued to correspond for another six months, and he asked me to marry him. I got on a train in February and went to Colorado, and we got married at a justice of the peace. My daughter was with my mother and dad, so she could finish fourth grade.

All I knew about him was what my brother told me, which turned out to be untrue. He told me about the big farm that he had in Tennessee and was making all of these wonderful plans for me and my little girl. I should not have been so trusting. So, now I am married again and back home working and hoping for the war to end and waiting for him to come home. After about eight months, I had saved enough money to buy a train ticket and go to Wyoming where he was stationed. I was only there a short time until it was quite apparent that he had a drinking problem.

From Wyoming, my brother and my husband got reassigned to a base in Colorado in 1945. We drove to Colorado in my brother's car. My daughter remained in Pennsylvania with my parents, since I knew this would be temporary.

I was not satisfied just to sit at home while in Colorado, so I got a job at a Safeway grocery store in the meat department. Everything went fine, until people started coming in and asking for tripe. I had no idea what tripe was, but I figured it was some kind of fish. So, I would say, "We do not have any tripe today." Until one day, a lady came in and asked for tripe, and I said, "No, our fish order will not be in until this afternoon." She just about jumped over the counter at me and told me that she did not want fish and that tripe was not fish. So, I said to the manager, "This lady wants tripe and we don't have any." He said, "Yes, we do. We always keep that under the ice." Meat was rationed so everyone wanted fish or anything that they could use as a substitute. Food and gasoline were rationed with stamps at that time. Tripe was not a rationed food. It was not considered something that you needed food stamps for. It turned out that tripe was pig stomach, and I had never heard it called that before. I was born and raised on a farm and, when we had a pig stomach to sell, we called it pig stomach, not "tripe." The manager got a good laugh about that, and I was off the hook.

Not long after that, they put me in charge of ordering and making sure we had an ample supply of Gerber's baby food. When the store manager saw that I was good with numbers and ordering strategies, he put me in charge of ordering inventory for the whole store. I had to make sure that we had every kind of food and that it was properly displayed. This was not a hard job, as the products from the store were all listed in long pages that you could flip through. Cigarettes were at the very top of one of the pages. Well after four weeks, the cigarettes did not come in, and we discovered it was because I had not seen them at the top of the page, so I had not checked them. I also was not a smoker, so it wasn't a priority for me, and they were overlooked. Our customers were livid because cigarettes were in short supply because they were mostly being shipped overseas to our soldiers at war. So you see, I have made my share of screw ups. My manager was very forgiving of my mistakes and just asked me to be more careful. I stayed on that job until my parents came to visit and were bringing my daughter with them. I asked for a few days off so that I could visit with them and tour the area. They would not give me the days off, so I quit the job.

My parents and aunt and uncle, along with my little girl and my younger sister and her little girl, all piled into my 1939 Oldsmobile that I had left behind and drove to Colorado. They stayed a week because my brother and his wife and his little girl lived there also. They all went home by train and left my car and my daughter, so she could go to school there. I was so busy with her any time that I had off from work that I did not notice that the drinking problem was getting worse with my husband.

One night, when it became very late, I went out looking for him and found him at a bar very intoxicated. I got him out of there and home to bed. It wasn't long after that he was sent to the state of Washington for some more training. I was left alone with my little girl. I got a job in a department store selling jewelry and worked there until the war was over. I really enjoyed that job.

When he came back from Washington, I met him at the train station, and he did not even have the ten cents that it would take for us to ride home on the trolley. Fortunately, I did have the money.

It was shortly after he came back that I became pregnant with my second child. I was about four months pregnant when the war ended.

CHAPTER 17

The "Island"

WHEN THE END of the war came, and it was time to pack all of our belongings and head East, my brother and brother-in-law were all discharged before my husband, so they got home first. Of course, by the time I got home, my parents' big house was full, and my house that I still owned was rented, so there was no place for me to live.

Fortunately, my father had bought an island of 14 acres that housed a big, old grist mill that he wanted to dismantle and sell the lumber. My dad told me that I could live in a house that he had bought as an investment property. Lumber was scarce then and much in demand, and my dad was going to dismantle the lumber from the grist mill and sell it, so it was a good investment.

In exchange for the use of the house, I let my father's hired man stay with us while he worked to dismantle the grist mill to sell the lumber. Lumber was so scarce during that time that news of the available lumber was spread by word of mouth. As Mr. Fry tore down the mill, he would stack the lumber in a pile. People came several times a week to buy lumber by the truckload if they were building a house or whatever. When they came and picked out the lumber, it was loaded on their truck, and Mr. Fry would come up to the house. I would go out with the measuring stick, and we had a formula to measure the lumber by the width, thickness and length of the boards to calculate the price for the lumber.

When I moved onto the island in 1945, after the Second World War was over, I thought it was to be a temporary place to live. Little did I know that this was to be the place that I was to "grow where I was planted" for the next 35 years until my retirement in 1980, when I was 65 years of age.

The property was only accessible over an old steel overhead bridge that was built around 1850 and had a plank floor. The two streams that surround the island are Fishing Creek and Cedar Run. They combined and split at the top end of the island and joined again at the bottom end of the island. The only way to get onto the island was over the old steel overhead bridge with a horizontal plank floor. It was great for me because it always rumbled to let me know when anyone was coming onto the island.

There was a house for the owner and a house for the man who managed the mill. The owner kept his house, but the other house and barn went with the sale of the property to my father. What a surprise and an eye opener that was. The weeds were as high as the window sills, and the yard had been used as a garbage dump. Apparently, when they opened a can of anything, they just opened the back door and out it went. We also were "lucky" because the toilet was at the end of a long path. The house was two stories with a kitchen, dining room and living room and one large bedroom and two small bedrooms upstairs. It was all furnished with discarded furniture, since my furniture was still at my parents' house and was all being used by my other family members, who were now staying there.

It was November, and staying warm was a problem. We had a kitchen range and a potbellied stove in the middle of the living room. The kitchen looked like it was added on as an afterthought to the house. It had a big old range that we used for heat, cooking and heating water if we wanted to wash dishes, clothes or take a bath. We were camping out. That was for sure. We did have electricity, but the light fixtures were wires hanging in the middle of the room with a light bulb hanging at the end. The electricity did serve another purpose. It pumped water into an old tin sink when we punched a button. When we had enough water, we punched the button again and the water stopped flowing. If we wanted warm water, we had to heat it on the stove in a big pot. I had a scrub board and tub to do the family laundry. The refrigerator was an "icebox." The floors were bare rough planks, and the kitchen floor had a cheap linoleum covering with most of the pattern worn off.

The outside of the house was made of wide planks with a strip of lumber covering the cracks, which they call board and batten. The inside of the walls were bare horsehair plaster. Later on, after I bought the island from my father, we tore the make-shift kitchen off and started to make repairs and build a new kitchen. Under the wall board, we found the walls insulated with old newspapers dated 1884 and 1885, so we assumed the addition must have been built around that timeframe. I am not sure when the original structure was built. We put up studding and plaster board to build the new kitchen.

Come Christmas, we were housebound because my husband had gotten the mumps, and I was pregnant. What a mess! My parents did come later in the day and bring us some Christmas dinner.

Now, I suppose everyone is wondering what this wonderful man that I married was doing? His drinking problem was continuing to get worse. Trying to get an alcoholic to be much help around the place was next to an impossible job, but things progressed and I was managing to make ends meet.

One evening, very early in my second marriage, while living on the island, I was sitting in front of the stove to keep warm. I think, unconsciously, I was waiting for my husband to come home. I crocheted, until way into the night at about midnight or later, when he came home. He was very abusive at night when he was drunk. Mr. Fry was still living with us because the grist mill had not been completely dismantled. Mr. Fry could hear the abuse from my husband, and he told me that he had a hard time not coming down to my defense. I do not know what happened to him after his job with my father was done. I don't think he was much younger than my father, but he was in much better health than my father.

Another time, while I was pregnant with my second child, my husband came home drunk and started beating on me. I ran out the front door for the neighbor's house. As I went out to the road, he threw stones at me, and I was fortunate that I could keep out of range. I was such a wreck that the neighbor thought that a hot bath would calm me down. It did do the trick, and I stayed until I saw him leave again before returning. When he came home again, I had taken my daughter and locked us in a bedroom so we were safe. We didn't know what he did the rest of the night.

Another time, my husband came home one night, drunk as could be, and was throwing up all over the bed. I was still pregnant with my second daughter. I took my first daughter, who was about ten years old, and the one chamber pot that we owned and locked us in another room. Sometime later, he started pounding on the door saying that he needed to use the chamber pot. Not wanting to open the door, I told him he would have to go use the outhouse at the end of the path. During the night, we could look out our window and see the outhouse. Suddenly, we heard my husband going down the stairs and out the back door. We kept watching, and he was naked as a jay bird but for a shirt that he kept trying to pull down to cover his manhood. We laughed about that but still stayed in our locked room. In the morning, we found the bedroom a complete mess. He had thrown up all over the bed and the floor and had slept in it.

The day before that, I had given the house a thorough cleaning, so this made me more than upset. I was mad! That was when we were still doing wash on a washboard and still hanging the wash on the clothesline to dry. I was doing all of the laundry in a galvanized tub set on a bench. This life I was living was almost like I imagine the homesteaders did as the West was being settled. I did have some advantages, however.

I said, "Now that you have made the mess, you will also clean it up." I gathered up the dirty linens and threw them out in the yard and told him to get the tub, heat the water and start scrubbing. I still do not know how I got away with that but, sure enough, he did as he was told and soon had a clothesline full of towels, bed linens and, of course, his clothes. When he got done with that, I reminded him that the room still had to be cleaned, and that took the rest of the day, but my day had been ruined.

I was to have my mother and aunt that next day for quilting. While my husband was still sleeping, I put my daughter in the car at about six in the morning and drove to my mother's and aunt's to tell them what had happened and that the quilting could not be held at my home.

In my way of thinking, this would be a lesson and maybe he would see the error of his ways and reform. Of course, he apologized and said he was turning over a new leaf. This was one of many leafs that he turned, until the final chapter and final page had been turned. The lesson he was supposed to have learned backfired on me because he said that because I was not compassionate and didn't clean up his messes that it made him worse. That comment rolled off my back like water rolls off a duck's back, and life went on.

It was in February 1946 that reality finally hit. I began to realize that instead of being "kept" that I was the "keeper." My husband had gotten a job at Piper Aircraft, but he was drinking up every pay check, leaving very little for the family. I was expecting a baby in April, so I was not able to seek employment.

Original island bridge looking across the bridge from my house to our neighbor on the hill across the road.

The dam on Fishing Creek on the front side of the island. This dam was built to divert water down a "race" on the right side of the stream to turn the water wheel at the grist mill when it was in operation in the 1890s.

Original island home with the early addition on the left.

Island home after exterior remodel in 1963.

CHAPTER 18

Not Your Average "Chick"

When I realized that I would have to be the "bread winner" in my marriage, I started to explore my options.

As you will discover as you read through my business beginnings, I wore many hats, "a one woman show," if you will. In today's world, I would have held the following positions: CEO, CFO, COO, Poultry Producer, Operations Manager, Billing Manager, Purchasing Agent, Marketing Manager, Sales Manager, Route and Transportation Manager, H.R. Manager, Exterminator, Inventor, and, sometimes, S.O.B.

I met up with a cousin, and she knew that things were not going so well, and she told me what she did when she needed extra money several years earlier. What she wanted to do was sell me her equipment that she no longer wanted to use. The idea was to get little day-old chicks and raise them for the farmers, so that when they were eight to ten weeks old, they could be put out to pasture to finish maturing by fall when they would be laying eggs. Since I was raised on a farm, this idea sounded like something that I could handle. I bought the brooding covers from her and ordered 500 day-old chicks. We drove 80 miles away to a hatchery and bought the first 500 chicks and brought the chicks back by car. The peeps were in cardboard cartons that were about 48 x 48 inches, and the carton was sectioned off with dividers holding about 25 peeps per section. I figured that would give me an opportunity to work at home and still take good care of my family.

The first 12 weeks of raising the new chicks went fine, but I had something to learn: that it was only a spring-time project. That lesson started me on the long road to success. I had no idea that this endeavor was to be my way of life for the balance of my working years. I got the chicks in February, and I still do not know how they survived for the ten days that I was in the hospital having my second daughter in early April, but when I returned home, there were very few fatalities.

All went well and, after my baby was born, it was time to advertise the chickens I had to sell. Within a few hours after the ad came out, the chicks had all found new homes, and I was ahead $300 dollars. For eight weeks, I felt like this was the kind of business I could handle. So, I sent to Sears & Roebuck and ordered another brooder, which doubled my capacity for raising peeps. I ordered 1,000 baby chicks from the hatchery, and they came via parcel post to the post office.

I got a call from the post office, and they said I had to come down right away and get the peeps (another name for baby chicks) because they were making quite a racket and driving them crazy. They were in cardboard boxes like my first batch. I had hired young men, who were working part-time to earn money to go to college. They were unloading the chicks out of the boxes one at a time. They were afraid that they would hurt the baby chicks. I told them that they were not baby chicks, just dollar bills. So, they just turned the boxes over gently, and the peeps scurried away.

It is a good thing that the building I was using for this enterprise would not hold more, or I probably would have bought more. Now, it is May, and I have 1,000 day-old chicks. All went fine until eight weeks later when I advertised, and I did not get one call. The chicks keep eating and growing, and soon I had a building with wall-to-wall chickens. What I did not know about the business was that the farmers only wanted the chicks in the spring. In desperation, I called my father and told him my problem. He always called me "Girlie" until the day he died. So, he said, "Girlie, what can I do?"

There was an old barn on the property, and it did not have steps to a second floor, nor any flooring. Mr. Fry was still dismantling the grist mill, so Dad came up with a plan. (At this point it was still Dad's property.) The mill had flooring that could be dismantled and used to put a floor in the second story of the old barn. So, Mr. Fry brought up the truck with lumber, and we started. As I look back, I do not know just how we did do it, but we put up the stairs and started the flooring. Each day as we finished, we put down hay and stretched wire to keep the chicks in and carried down what we thought the space would accommodate. After a week's hard work, the chicks had a nice new home. All went well, and I found a feed man that would sell me feed on credit until I could sell the chicks. I paid as much along as I could, which was very little.

I had my rent money from the house I had built in 1939, and what I could salvage from my husband's paycheck from Piper Aircraft.

Things went along fine until, one day, I went to feed the chickens and found eggs all over the floor. So, I called Dad again and told him what was happening. He said, "No problem. Just nail up a board, put another one across the front, and cut some short ones and space those about 12 inches apart to make nests." Living on a farm, I did know what a nest should look like so, once again, I am a carpenter. My dad sent me some "china eggs" to put in the nests so that the chickens would get the hang of what was expected of them. They were quick learners, and soon I was knee deep in eggs. I sold a few locally and a few dozen to a little market in town, but I had lots and lots more eggs. I had heard of some other farmers in the area that produced eggs, so I called on them and asked how they sold their eggs. One of these farmers was the agriculture agent for the County. After he heard my story, he said that he would visit periodically to see how I was doing with the chicken business. From talking with this man and other farmers, it turned out that an outfit from Bradford, Pennsylvania came around every week and would buy the eggs. They furnished the crates to carry them in, so now I am in the egg business. I was selling four or five cases a week and was doing quite well, along with keeping the little store supplied and some locals that would stop. I also delivered from door-to-door if that was necessary.

The agriculture agent came by one day and said that I was feeding a lot of chickens that were not producing eggs. It seemed that then it was time for them to be killed and sold for food. What did I know about "culling chickens," as he called it? Well, the good man told me what to do. You checked to see if the hens were losing their feathers around their heads and if they were going into a molt, which meant that they would not be laying any more eggs for an extended time. You catch the chicken by its feet, turn it upside down and lay three fingers between the pelvic bones and, if they fit, that meant that the chickens were still producing eggs. The chicken's life was saved for a while and, if the three fingers did not fit, it was put in a corn crib for holding to be slaughtered later.

At this point, I felt I needed a job to bring in more income. I applied at Sylvania, which was one of my former employers. They had just built a new plant near my home. My alcoholic husband said, "Who would hire you?" They hired me right away. I worked the 11 p.m. to 7 a.m. shift so I could keep my small poultry business going during the day. I hired a woman to take care of my girls while I slept in the morning.

After two months, I had to quit this job because I was falling asleep on the job. The foreman would wake me and take me outside for a walk in the night air to wake me up. One night, I was dreaming that I was putting a barrette in my oldest daughter's hair before she went to school. I was making "getters" for light bulbs and, when the foreman woke me up, I had a metal "getter" in my mouth. I was trying to open it as if I was putting the barrette in her hair.

CHAPTER 19

My Second Daughter, Pat

IN EARLY APRIL, my husband took me to my parents and then on to the Jersey Shore hospital for the delivery of my second daughter. She came at nine o'clock the next morning. My husband did not come to see us until 7:30 p.m. that night. He did not work that day but spent the day at a bar, celebrating the birth of his child. Years later, I found out that he was at a bar with another woman.

I have no regrets because my daughter was born, and she has been a joy in my life. Her sister was 11 years old, and she was just the best little mother that a baby could have. She loved her and all of her free time was spent playing with her and, one day, she undertook bathing her while I was out in the garden. She did just fine, but at first it gave me a fright.

I knew if I wanted to have any money, I had to hide a little away whenever I had extra. Eventually, I accrued $600, which I kept hidden in my Bible for safekeeping. In the spring of 1947, the stores in the nearby town of Lock Haven were having their fur coat sales. I went down and looked at the coats and found a beautiful golden-side muskrat coat. The going price was $800.00. I tried it on several times and then went across the street to a store where I had looked at coats before. The sales lady said arrogantly, "Are you going to buy a coat this time, or are you just looking?" She had to go upstairs to bring down a coat. I said, "Don't bother, I'm just looking." I went back across the street and tried on the $800 coat again. I just could not see myself going home without it. I said to the salesman, "I'll bet if somebody would lay $500 on the table, they could get this coat." He said, "You better believe it!" So, I opened up my pocketbook and laid down $500, which I had been saving for just such a special event as this. Well, that salesman was really surprised because he had just lost a large sale on the coat due to the greatly reduced price that he had agreed to for cash. He also sold coats to my sister and, when he saw her, he told her what I had done. He was really put out by the outcome of that sale.

I went out of my old dilapidated house all dressed up in my fur coat and looked like a prosperous person. The house I was living in did not give the same impression!

Pat, age 3.

My girls, age 16 and 5.

Pat, age 6, holding our Chihuahua, Tinker, in front of our 1952 Chevy station wagon and 1936 washing machine on the porch.

Pat's college graduation photo.

Pat in 2013.

CHAPTER 20

Rats, Rats Everywhere

AROUND THIS SAME timeframe, I realized that we had an infestation of wharf rats on the island. These rats were much larger than the ordinary rat. There were not any in or around my house because there was nothing for them to eat. We discovered the rats when we found rat holes in the chicken coops and, eventually, we saw rats running through the barn. To get rid of the rats, we rented a small concrete mixer and put in 40 pounds of hamburger and mixed it with strychnine. A hired man put this mixture out in small amounts all around the buildings and anywhere he thought the rats might run. After a few days, we were able to pick up bushel baskets full of rats. My husband went to the lower end of the island and dug a hole and buried the rats. That ended the rat problem.

CHAPTER **21**

The Next Step

THEN CAME THE broiler industry in the South, and the price of live poultry plummeted. When I was quoted a price far below what I could afford to sell my chickens for, I just said, "No, thank you" and called a friend in the business and asked about a feather plucker. He was in the business, and he said that he just happened to have one in stock. I got in my car with my little girl and drove 80 miles, put the thing in my trunk and home I went to set this crude machine up in my basement. That was the only place that I had at the time.

Now that I had learned how to "cull" the chickens and had solved the rat problem, I needed to learn how to slaughter the chickens.

I killed and dipped the chickens outside in a little building that stood close to the house and carried them through an outside entrance to the picking machine. You held chickens by their feet over the rotating drum of rubber fingers that did a good job of removing the feathers. Then, I took them up to my kitchen and finished getting them ready for market. That was the start of the business of killing the non-layers to make the business more profitable.

When I was growing up on the farm, my dad put the chicken's head on a chopping block and cut the chicken's head off with an ax. The chicken flopped around in the yard until it was dead. I knew that I could never hit where I aimed with that ax, so the man suggested that I hang them on the clothesline, put the knife on their neck, turn my head, cut the throat, and take off running because the chicken would thrash around and cover me with blood. Then, I had boiling water and dipped the chickens in it to loosen the feathers and, after the de-feathering job, the hard part came. You had to cut it open and take out the entrails (internal organs of the chicken).

Since it meant money in my pocket, I had no problem with any of this after a while. It was not long until I realized that using the clothesline for killing the chickens was not going to work as the demand began to get larger. I still could not look at the poor things as I cut their throats, so I decided that a wooden barrel with a notch cut in the top would work. I could hold the chicken by its head, put it in the notch, place the knife on its throat, turn my head, and take off the head. The chicken would fall into the barrel and would be ready for the hot water bath.

In the early phase of my business, which was killing chickens and getting them ready for market, I started out with one chicken and, not knowing what to do with the entrails, I went down in the woods and dug a hole to bury them. This seemed like a perfect solution to my problem, so I finally got my husband to dig me a ditch, and each time that I killed a couple of chickens, I would put the entrails in the ditch and covered them up. This went on for quite a while and, one day when I went down to bury more entrails, the ground in the ditch was moving. I knew then that this was no longer going to work because the flies had found a perfect place for their maggots to breed. Now, I had to think of a different solution for the disposal of the entrails. Finally, I said to myself, why don't I get some pigs to eat the entrails because pigs don't have a gourmet appetite and will eat anything? The foundation to the old grist mill that my father had torn down was still there, and it was about 12 feet deep and high enough to keep the pigs confined. They seemed more than happy to eat all the entrails I could feed them at that time in my business. I had a young man working for me that I thought a lot of, and he was a hard worker and very conscientious. His name was Glen. One evening, after quitting time, I saw Glen come flying back across the bridge. He went right down to the plant and, when I saw him coming back up, I asked him why he came back in such a hurry. He said, "Well, Mrs. Warren, I forgot to feed the pigs." Glen was another great employee early on in my business.

My husband was still in the picture, but the drinking was getting worse. I had to hide the baby's milk and formula at night if I wanted to be sure that I would have any for her in the morning. My husband would come in drunk and drink any milk that he could find.

When my youngest daughter was about three or four, he was going into town one day, and he wanted her to go with him. He didn't come back for a long time. I finally went down to our small town and went to the drugstore and asked them if they had seen anything of my little girl. The druggist said, "Yes, she is sitting over there in the corner by the funny book rack." Her dad was next door at the beer joint. She had been there for several hours, but she was content because she was looking at all the funny books. After that, I did not allow her to go with him because I never could be sure of what he was telling me about where he was really going.

Then, I realized that the little bit of money I was making was disappearing little by little. I did not realize just how bad it was until I went to the A & P store and tried to write a check and was told that I no longer had check writing privileges on that account. This was money that I had deposited in the account from the egg business. I was really mad, and I told the clerk to hold my groceries until I came back. I went to the bank and asked to talk with the president of the bank. I told him that my name was on that account, and I wanted money to buy groceries. By the time I got back to the grocery store, the bank president had called the store and told them to cash my check.

Being the dummy that I was, I had the account in both names. My husband had gone to the bank and told them that I was not allowed to have any more money. Shortly after that incident, I withdrew the money from that bank and took it to another bank in the next town. I put this new account in only my name.

It was at that time that I was beginning to realize that keeping the family and educating the children was going to be my responsibility. I was getting no help from my husband.

We had undertaken remodeling the house and moved the stove into the dining room along with the kitchen sink. This was truly camping. The door to the outside had a screen door on it, so it was convenient to put the milk between the door and screen. That door could not be used since it dropped to the basement level, so all during this time we only had one outside door.

This went on for about a year, and my husband decided that he would leave. So he went back to Tennessee where he was born and stayed for about three months. In that time, my father had sold all of the lumber from his grist mill investment and he said, "Girly, if you want to buy the island, I will sell it to you for $1,500." So I said, "OK, I will buy it, but I don't have the money right now." My father still put the place in my name. A year after that, I was able to sell my first house I built for $8,000 that I had only paid $3,700 for, so then I was able to repay my father the $1,500. The rest of that money was how I got started in the chicken business. I realized that I was going to have to rely on myself for a living for myself and my children. Eventually, my husband came back and tried to make amends. I said, "No, I am not interested." He then said, "If you don't let me come back, I am going to jump off the bridge at Lock Haven and kill myself." Well, I guess in hindsight, that would've been the best solution to the problem. Anyway, I took him back, and he finally said to me one day, "If I had known you only had $10,000, I never would've married you." Then, he also said that the reason he married me was because he was drunk. But anyway, I used the rest of that money, or most of it, to start the business. This was after he had turned another page in the book.

CHAPTER 22

Business Expansion

ABOUT THIS TIME a large local chain of grocery stores decided that they needed to sell fancy dressed poultry and contacted me. This was big business for me. I knew that I no longer could do all of this in the small confines of my basement and kitchen, so I contracted to have a building put up to accommodate this operation.

I built a one story concrete block building, approximately 30 x 20 feet next to the original barn. About two years later, a state inspector came to my business and told me that I would have to add another room onto this building in order to separate the slaughtering room from the eviscerating room to be in compliance with state regulations. I added this onto the back of my existing concrete block building.

Not having enough money to hire a babysitter, and my oldest daughter going to school, I would put the baby on a pillow and carry her to the building that was to be the beginning of The Island Poultry Farm, Inc.

I built a shelf on the wall in the room where I was working that was about four feet high and two feet wide, so I could put my baby and her pillow on the shelf while I worked.

As the business progressed, I needed a freezer and a walk in cooler, so I added another big room, this time in the front of the original concrete block building. I had to add a second story to accommodate storage space.

Shortly after this addition, the State told me that I had to have two restrooms in the facility. Prior to this time, my employees were using my home bathroom, so I added another room on the side of the building to accommodate a furnace and the two restrooms. I also added office space for myself and my secretary. This meant that I had to tear down the original old barn, where I first raised my chickens, because I had to make space for the addition.

Fancy dressed poultry was in demand and, after one year, I was in the chicken slaughtering business for good, and the egg business was no more.

One day, when I was working in the new plant, the phone rang. It was my husband screaming, "Come quick, Jean is trying to kill me." I ran to the house to find the kitchen floor covered with sugar, and my husband with a piece of glass from the broken sugar bowl sticking out of the side of his head. It seems that he was calling me some pretty fowl names, and this did not sit well with my daughter, Jean, so she picked up the first thing close at hand and bailed it at him. It was a year later, and we were still finding sugar above the window frames. From then on, he was very careful around my older daughter.

I did not know how much he respected her fighting power until we were out picking up a big load of live chickens and he was drunk as usual, which I could not understand because I had been with him, I thought, at all times. I didn't know that he had a bottle stashed behind the seat in the truck and, as we were loading chickens, he was also getting loaded. When we started home with the chickens, we had close encounters with seven cars because he kept punching my left arm while he was trying to drive drunk. My left arm felt as if every muscle had been crushed from him punching me. When I had taken all of the abuse I could stand, I grabbed the keys from the truck, and we came to a dead stop right on the highway. I jumped out and went around to the driver's side and opened the door and ordered him out. He objected to this, so I took off my shoe and started hitting him on the head with my shoe. Several cars passed, and I have no idea what they thought was going on, but no one stopped. After I got him out of the truck, I got in and started the truck and would have left him by the side of the road, but he managed to get in the passenger's side. He was very meek from there on home. All of the while, he was pleading for me not to tell my daughter. It was really funny at the time because, when we drove in, he ran in the house and got a pan and dashed to the cellar for potatoes to fix for dinner. That was a quiet evening, and Jean did not find out what had happened to make him be so helpful and pleasant until much later. She must have thought that he had really turned over a new leaf. That only lasted until the next day when he could get away to the beer garden again. I went to the bank the next day to deposit some money, and the bank president saw me enter. I did not realize that my blouse sleeve did not cover all of the bruising on my left arm where my husband had been beating my arm while he was driving the truck the night before. He asked me how I got the bruising on my arm, and I told him that I fell down the stairs. He commented, "Sure you did!"

It was a small town and, by then, I guess most people knew I was having a rough time with my husband.

Original barn to which I added a second floor and, eventually, the addition on the left side where I slaughtered poultry.

Pat cleaning her first chicken at age 2 in 1948.

CHAPTER 23

Lice, Those Lousy Lice

WHEN I SAW how much money I could make, I needed more chickens than I could produce, so I bought from local farmers and was really in business.

One time, I bought some chickens from a local farmer and put them in the same pen with the 1,000 chickens I already had, not knowing that they were infested with lice. Shortly after introducing these chickens to my original chickens, they started losing weight and were starting to look like skin and bone. I picked one up to look more closely at it, when I noticed there was something wrong with them. I discovered lice crawling on the chicken skin when I separated the feathers. I knew if I did not do something to treat the lice, the chickens would not mature, and I would lose the entire building of chickens.

I went to the neighborhood druggist to find out what I should use to treat the lice. To take care of this problem, I had to use Black Leaf 40, a substance that is high in nicotine, and the druggist warned me that it was very toxic and to take precautions when using the product. I had to place a dropper of the liquid on the chicken's rear end. Since I was warned that you could have a reaction from this product, I told the young men who were helping me with this treatment, David and Kit, to catch the chickens and hand them to me at arm's length. Before hand, we made a wire enclosure to separate the treated chickens from the untreated chickens and, as the boys handed a chicken to me, I treated it and dropped it into the treated pen area, until we had them all treated. Together we treated 1,000 chickens that night, one at a time. We finished about 12 o'clock at night, and I sent the boys home.

Shortly after they left, I became very ill. When I laid down on the bed, I felt like I was falling into a chasm. Then, I started violently throwing up. It was fortunate that my mother was staying with me at the time. She called the doctor and told him that I had been poisoned. He thought that I had taken a poison as a way of ending my life, so he and his wife came running to take care of me. They had just flown in from New York and were still both in their evening clothes when they arrived at my house. He gave me an injection of strychnine to counteract the nicotine that I had inhaled and absorbed through my skin. By this time, it was 1:00 a.m. and my husband came in dead drunk. The doctor flew into my husband and he yelled, "I want you to sit by this woman and keep her awake all night." Of course, my mother also sat with me because she had no confidence that a drunk could take care of me. The next day, I seemed to be OK.

In a few weeks, the chickens again showed signs of lice, and I went through the same procedure and became very sick again. My mother again called the doctor, and he gave me another shot with the same instructions to keep me awake all night. He also told me not to do that again because he was not sure that he could save my life, if I got exposed again. I don't know why I never thought to wear a mask or wear some kind of protective gloves. Guess I must have thought I was invincible, especially the second time!

Another time, very early in the business, right after we had gotten a large grocery store account and we were not automated yet, I sent out an order with my husband to deliver. We were so small a business at this point that the only truck that we had or needed was our pickup truck. The order was to be delivered to a store in Montoursville, Pennsylvania. On the way, he had to go through a small town called Newberry. There was a tavern on the street that he had to pass. He stopped at the tavern and forgot to come out to deliver the chickens until after the flies had gotten at them. Before he got home that night, I had a call from the store saying to come back and get the chickens that they were crawling with maggots. So, I sent him back and that whole order had to be buried. Not only did he come home late, but he came home with a little dog in his shirt pocket. The little dog was so small that he fit in a tea cup. It was the runt of the litter, and the tavern owner gave it to him. At least that is the story I was told. We named him Tinker (short for Tinker Bell because he fit in a tea cup), and he grew up to be a sweet little dog. He spent many years with me, and he gave great comfort to Aunt Edna, who lived with us off and on over the years. (More about Aunt Edna later in the story.) She spent many hours just holding him on her lap. I'm sure, when she was not there that he missed her. Tinker lived for 14 years, and he finally died of lung cancer.

CHAPTER **24**

Another Business Expansion

AFTER TWO YEARS of buying chickens locally and slaughtering them for market, I decided that since I knew how to raise chickens to slaughter, I would build a new three story building to raise 8,000 chickens at a time to slaughter.

I told the agricultural agent what I was planning to do, and he said, "Don't you think you are getting a little big for your britches?" Of course, that made me even more determined to go forward with the project.

It was 1951 when I was talking with some carpenters about building the large three story building for me to further expand my business. My five-year-old daughter was standing nearby, and she started telling me how she would walk out on the foundation beams that still remained on the grist mill foundation. They were about eight inches wide and covered with slippery moss. I did not know that she had been doing this, so I said, "Honey, please don't do that anymore. One of these days, you're going to fall in." Well, being a strong-willed child and wanting to show me that she could cross the beams without falling, she decided to go out on the beams while I was standing there talking with the carpenters. But, wouldn't you know, when she was about halfway across one of the beams, down she fell right into the pig wallow. I turned to see her fall and jumped down into the pig wallow. She was lucky that the pigs had decided that they needed a place that would hold water for them to roll around in when they were hot. They had displaced the brick floor of the grist mill to make their wallow, so she fell right in the middle of their pig wallow. When I realized that she was OK, I gave her a smack on her rump through her muddy, wet bib overalls and told her to get to the house and get cleaned up. She cried all the way to the house. As she passed the neighbor's home on the way to our house, the neighbor asked her what was wrong. She sobbed, "I fell into the pig wallow, and Mom is really mad at me and told me to go get cleaned up." I actually was not mad at her as much as I was scared for her and then relieved that she was OK. She was a sensitive child, and all I had to do was raise my voice an octave for her to think I was upset with her. She never got into much trouble as a child.

After we had agreed on the price for the new building and how it was to be constructed, I went ahead with the project. I built a three story building 30 x 80 feet. By the time the building was completed in about two months, I had enough chickens to fill that new building.

There was another family that lived about 12 miles from me, who decided to get into the chicken raising business because I was in the business, and it looked like I was making money. The husband came to my building site one day and said that the building would not stand for more than two years because of the cinder block construction. He built his out of concrete blocks. He was out of business in two years because he didn't think raising chickens would require much effort. My three story cinder block building was later turned into my processing plant and is still standing as of 2014. His building had deteriorated over the years and looked ramshackle the last time I saw it years ago.

This was a very challenging business and it was new to me, so I had to learn as I went along. Sometimes, it was a very costly learning experience.

Realizing how much work it was going to be to feed and water the chickens, I bought automatic feeding and watering systems. I discovered that I still was not able to do all of the work, so I hired a young man who was a junior in high school, to help me. He was a very good worker. My husband decided that he wanted to test a new electric brooder that was being promoted by the power company in our area. The power company came in and set up two brooders on loan for the testing.

The next morning, the man taking care of the chickens came rushing to my house and said that chickens were dying, and he had found 25 dead so far. He did not know what to do to keep more from dying. I rushed to the chicken house with him, and we immediately unplugged the brooders. The brooders were very hot on one side, and the chickens were crowding to the opposite side of the brooder and were smothering each other. We sent the test brooders back and put in the original brooders that worked just fine, and we had no further problems with brooders.

Another time, my husband was drinking a lot and, one day very early in the morning, he came home and went down to the chicken house. I was never sure why he went there. He opened all of the windows on both sides of the building, which caused a cross breeze.

Within the next couple of days, when I went to check on the chickens, I noticed that chickens were wheezing and some had died. I decided to take some of the dead chickens to a laboratory about 80 miles from my house to have them analyzed and determine the cause of the problem, so I could hopefully medicate the flock to prevent further carnage.

I did not want to drive all that way by myself, so I asked one of my employees, who was like a son to me, to ride along with me. As we were driving and talking, he said to me, "You know what the matter is with you?" I said, "No." He said, "You are a Chevrolet trying to go like a Cadillac." I did not know what he meant by this statement, and I never asked. I will always remember his unusual statement.

The lab determined that the chickens had some kind of bronchial infection. After I got back home, I called a local distributor, who sold medications for animals. They sent over their representative, who dealt with poultry diseases and we met in my office, which was in my house at this time. I told him about the symptoms and he said, "Let's go down to the chicken house, so I can see the flock." As we left the house and started down the road to the chicken house, my nosey neighbor stuck her head out her screen door and yelled, "Did you have a good time with your boyfriend while you were in the house?" I did not think her question should be dignified with an answer, so I ignored her. Since I was in a male dominated business and had to meet all of my business associates in my home office, she must have thought I had a lot of boyfriends!

After he looked over the flock, he agreed with the lab that the problem was a bronchial infection and that I would have to medicate the water that the chickens drank. I bought a solution and put one-third of the bottle in each of my large water barrels that fed water into the drinking troughs. This was a problem that was contagious, so I had to use this medication as long as I raised poultry in this building. I finally discovered that my husband had caused this problem in a drunken stupor the evening he opened all of the windows in the chicken house.

I decided that it was time to turn in the car and buy a Chevrolet station wagon that was to serve as a means for transporting my products and also as a family car. After working all day and feeding my family, I would take Jean and Pat and a couple of girlfriends of Jean's, and off we would go to the skating rink at Hecla Park. It was about 12 miles from where we lived. Jean loved to roller skate and took pleasure in helping her six-year-old sister learn to skate. I would take them in and stay until they had their skates on and watch them for a little while. Then, I would go back out in the car, where I had a pillow and blanket, and I would get in the back seat and sleep until they were ready to go home. After working hard all day and taking care of the many things necessary to keep things going smoothly, I would be exhausted and needed that few hours of rest. Of course, it wasn't long before the rumor started that I was not going there to sleep but was having an affair with some man.

One evening, my girlfriend and her husband came by to show

me their new car. They said, "Get in and we will take you for a ride." I said, "Jean drove up to the skating rink with her friends, so let's go there and watch them skate." When we got to the rink, the station wagon was no place to be seen. I did not know where Jean and her friends had gone. So, we came back home. I waited a while, and when she did not show up, I went to bed. Around 12 o'clock in the morning, the phone rang and it was somebody telling me that Jean had overturned the Chevy station wagon. I called my dear friend Ruth and asked her if she would take me to the accident site. Thank goodness, my daughter was not hurt. She said that a deer had run in front of her and that caused her to have the accident. I never said anything, but I did not believe that for a minute because she was coming around a sharp curve in the road too fast and caused the vehicle to overturn. I'm thankful that she was not hurt. Some men, who came along and saw the accident, helped to upright the station wagon. I got in the station wagon to drive it home and did not realize that, when it had upset, the battery acid had come out and was on the seat. That ruined the dress that I had on. The sad part was, I had just put on this dress that my mother had bought for me a few days earlier. It was the only store-bought dress that my mother had ever gotten me.

The business progressed and since I had built the larger chicken house to raise my own chickens for slaughter, the chickens that I did not need for my own business, I sold to a big processor and did quite well.

I kept on raising and killing my own poultry for about four years until the demand was so great that I had to seek an outside source for chickens to slaughter, and I discovered that along with buying chickens from local farmers, I could also buy from the Southern states.

I had two large black walnut trees on the island and an older man who worked for me asked if I was going to do anything with the walnuts that fell from the tree. I told him, "No." He asked if he could gather the walnuts, and that was fine with me. He would gather a couple bushels in a large pail. I don't know how he dried and shelled them, so he could crack open the nut to pick out the walnut meat.

Every year, for about four years, he would gather the walnuts and bring me a couple of pounds for a $1.00 a pound. I don't know what he charged others, but it did not seem like very much money per pound for all of the work he had to do to extract the walnut meat.

Many years later, a man came to the island and told me that he would give me $200 for each of the walnut trees. No one used the walnuts anymore, so I sold the trees to him and he came in and cut them down and took them away to be milled into black walnut lumber. Black walnut lumber was very precious and hard to find. Since one of these trees was sitting on the border of my neighbor's lot, I felt it was only fair to give her $100.

The three story chicken house.

A chicken brooder.

Round feed hopper in background and moving feeder trough on the floor.

My first business vehicle with advertisement on the door, 1954.

CHAPTER 25

End of Second Marriage

MY HUSBAND WAS working at Piper Aircraft full-time, but he would leave his job sometimes during the day and go to a bar. He would come home about the same time he should have been getting home from work. I could smell beer on his breath, but I figured he had just stopped for a beer after work. Finally, the company had enough of his behavior and he lost his job. In 1954, he saw advertised that civil service exams were to be held, so I suggested that he should take the exam. He did take the exam and passed it. This proved that he was not a dumb man, just addicted to alcohol. He got a part-time job delivering mail with our local post office with the stipulation that, if he was ever caught drinking while in postal uniform, he would no longer have a job. He took that threat seriously and did well in the job, although it was only part-time, so he had plenty of time for drink and enough money to support his habit. He never contributed one cent to the family from that day on, but he still had a room at the house and put his feet under my table at meal time, if he was home. He helped some in the early stages of the young business, but often I think that I would have been better off hiring outside help.

I discovered that he was also filling his vehicle from my company gas tank. I called the gas company and told them to quit delivering gas until further notice. This went on for about six weeks, and he finally said, "I know that you are not getting gas so that I cannot fill up my truck." I said, "Yes, what took you so long to figure that out?"

In 1955, he took off for Tennessee to visit his folks or so he said. When he came back, he called me when he was about 30 miles away to tell me that he had his mother with him. When she came in, she turned to him and said, "She even has the house clean." I never did find out what she had expected. She was there about three weeks and criticized every move that my oldest daughter made and did not like the food that I fixed. I had planned to go on a three day trip with my sister and her son and asked him if he would take care of the chickens while I was away. He seemed agreeable, but the next morning all hell broke loose, and his mother told me that she came up with him to see after his interests and that she wanted me to pack my belongings and leave. I said, "I think you have this all wrong. I will not be the one leaving." I had retained a lawyer some time before when he had beaten me so badly, so I just dialed his number and told him what was going on. He said, "When he comes home from the post office for lunch, you ask him how soon he can be gone." I did not tell his mother what I was told and, when my husband came home, she told him that I had the nerve to call a lawyer. I said, "Yes, and he wants to know how soon you two can be out of here." My husband said, "We are going right now." I said, "Fine! The children and I will be at the neighbor's until you are gone." That was the end of them, but things were still disappearing from the plant.

My husband knew that we had to keep our knives sharpened once or twice a day. The girls went down to the maintenance room to sharpen knives. The sharpener was missing, and I only knew of one way that it could have gotten away. I knew that he had to have taken it. I called the post office where he worked and got a hold of him and asked him if he had taken the sharpener. He confessed that he had the sharpener. I said, "I will give you one half hour to have that sharpener back here. If it is not here by then, the sheriff will be calling on you." Well, the sharpener was back within the half hour because he had a government job and, if the sheriff had showed up at the post office, he could have lost his job. He did everything possible to make my life miserable. I think the only thing that kept me sane was the fact that I had two children to raise and educate, which fortunately I was able to do.

After much abuse, trials and tribulations, he finally turned the last page of the book and he was gone, at least from my place. Each time he came in drunk and abusive, he would apologize and say that he was turning over a new leaf. Finally, I figured that the book was about full and I said, "The last page has been turned, and the book is closed."

A sad event also happened in that year in 1955. My dear sister-in-law, Helen, died in childbirth. She was like a sister to me and was actually better to me than my sisters were to me. She left two young girls, who were about nine and ten years old at the time. She and I had an agreement that when our daughters outgrew their clothes, especially coats, that we would swap clothes. This worked out well because her one daughter was younger than my daughter, and her other daughter was older than my daughter. This was such a sad time for her daughters, and I tried to help them with clothing and whatever else I could do at the time. They went to live with their mother's sister in a nearby town. Their aunt was a wonderful person, and I am happy to say that these lovely girls are beautiful women today, just like their dear mother. They both live in California.

In the spring of 1956, a man came to the door of the plant and asked for Mrs. Warren. I stopped working and asked him what I could do for him. He said, "I am from the IRS, and I came to audit your books." I said, "OK." I took him to the house because, at that time, I did not have an office and did everything at my kitchen table. I asked him if he would like to have a cup of coffee. He threw up his hands in the air and said, "You are not bribing me." I said, "OK, but I'm going to have a cup." So, I went and poured myself a cup of coffee. I got out the ledger and showed it to him. He said, "Who did this?" And I said, "I did," and he said he never saw books kept like that before. And I said, "Well, I'm not a bookkeeper, so this is the only way that I know how to keep the credits and debits." He scratched his head and began asking me questions.

My oldest daughter was in nursing school, and I gave her a $5.00 a month allowance. I knew that wasn't very much, but it was all I had. He said, "But, why would you ever give a girl a $5.00 allowance for a month when you don't have it to give?" He spent about one hour and a half asking about this $5.00 allowance and was keeping me away from my work, but I didn't say anything, and pretty soon after that he left. He was trying to imply that I was making more than I was claiming on my income tax return and could therefore easily give my daughter $5.00 and probably gave her more than I was claiming.

Not long after his first visit, he came back again. He asked to see my books again. I said, "Well, they will be the same as they were before only that I have added the current dealings." He asked me again, "How much did you give your daughter?" I told him it was the same amount as I told him the last time, and it had not changed. He said, "Are you sure it is the same amount?" and I said, "Yes, I am sure." He said he could not understand why I would give her $5.00. I told him it was all I had to give her. He studied the books for a while and asked me what the asset of $8.00 was that was labeled "junk." I told him it was for junk that I had sold. He said, "What is junk?" I told him it was scrap metal, etc. that I had laying around and sold to a scrap dealer. He said, "Well, you don't put that on a tax return."

He came back again after a few months and went through the same procedure and said, "Now, are you sure you only give your daughter $5.00 per month?" I said, "I'm sure as I can be and that hasn't changed." He left and, in another few months, back he came again. When he came, he was taking me away from my work and that was the way I was making my living, so I said to him, "I am not talking to you anymore. I've told you all that I am going to tell you. If you want to know anything more, you will have to go to the man who does my accounting." He could see that I was pretty riled up and he said, "Now, now, Mrs. Warren, don't get so upset. I just need you to sign this paper, and I came to tell you that we discovered that we owe you twenty-nine cents." I said to him, "I'm not going to sign your paper." It said that the audit had found everything to be exactly as they thought it would be. I wondered what that statement meant. If I had signed the paper, I felt they could have said that I owed them money or most anything. I said, "I am not a bookkeeper, nor am I a typist, but I do know how to punch the typewriter keys good enough to type a letter that I will sign." He said, "No, it has to be this letter." I said to him, "You can take your twenty-nine cents and stick it where the sun doesn't shine." I don't think I said those exact words. I am kind of ashamed to tell you what I really did say to him. I said again, "I am not going to talk to you anymore because you are getting paid for every minute you talk to me, and I am losing money for every minute that I talk to you."

I asked him, "Why did you decide to audit me?" He said, "Well, you were turned in." I said, "Well, who would do that?" He said, "I cannot disclose that information," and I said, "You don't need to disclose that information." I knew that it was my ex-husband, who had left the year before, who had turned me in. That's not the only thing that my ex-husband did to see how much trouble he could cause my business.

CHAPTER **26**

Life Post-Divorce

I THINK IT is about time that I tell about my very exciting life. Ha! Ha! After my husband was gone, I was fair game for gossip. I never was quite sure when or how it got started, but I think anyone reading this would come to the same conclusion that I did. My business was not far enough along for me to have an office outside the house, so all of my bookwork was done at the kitchen table after my children were in bed. When a salesman came to call, and we had things that needed to be discussed, I would take them to the kitchen to talk and sometimes I would offer them coffee, since that was what I practically lived on anyway. When we would finish our business, the man would leave, and I would go back to the plant to work. The neighbor from across the road would come out and say, "Did you and your boyfriend have a good time?" I was a little taken back but said that we had all of our business transacted. Well, that was just the way it went, until I was able to get an office in the front of the plant.

I had a lot of medical problems and, every couple of weeks, I would have a doctor's appointment, and he would give me Vitamin B-12 shots to keep me going. One day, when I went for my shot, he asked me if I knew who I was supposedly running around with now. I said, "No," and he seemed surprised and said, "You are running around with me." Then, he surprised me by saying that he was glad because they had finally gotten him with someone that was a lady worth something. I knew his wife real well, and she thought that this was all hilarious. On and on it went.

Sometime later, I stopped to see my very good friend and she said, "I am mad at you." I said, "Now what did I do?" She replied, "You have been going with this man from over in the other valley that has seven children." Now this was a surprise because I did not know anyone from the other valley, let alone one with seven children. She began to laugh because she knew that I did not have time for any dilly-dallying, even if I had a mind to.

On occasion, a salesman or one of the brokers would come in town and stay at the hotel for the night. We would go to the one nice restaurant in town, have dinner and discuss problems or strategies for selling products or for solving the ever so many problems that came up with the running of my business. I could see nothing wrong with having dinner and talking, but the next day I was questioned by the neighbor about the good time that I had.

My own family may have had something to do with this gossip also, though I do not really know. My husband and brother were drinking buddies and right after my husband and I broke up for good, I would get phone calls at two or three o'clock in the morning. There was always a lot of foul talk and saying what I needed was a good, the "F" word, and that he would be right there to take care of that. I would hear this commotion in the background and knew that the call was being made from a beer garden, and I also recognized the voice as my brother's. Needless to say, that was the end of that night's sleep because I did not know what might happen with them in their drunken state.

I also had a sister that liked to gossip and was coming to the neighbors but would not stop to see me. On one occasion, she accused me of running around with a married man. This was not the truth and that was the last day I had anything else to do with her. She was the one in the family that had a lot to live with, and I think that it made her feel better about herself if she thought that she could tear me apart.

CHAPTER **27**

SBA Loan

WHEN IT BECAME evident that I was going to have to expand my business again, I did not have the money. I went to the bank and tried to make a loan, and I was turned down. So, I tried another bank and was again rejected. I tried the third bank with no better results. I was determined that my project would work and that I was not about to give up. I had heard of the Small Business Administration and how you could get a loan from them if you had been turned down by three banks. I had already met that requirement. The last bank I went to with my request told me that he did not have time to talk to me then, but that I should come back at 7:00 that evening. I said, "You will not be open this evening." He was very polite and said, "I will be open for you." This did not sound quite right to me, so on the way home, I stopped at my girlfriend's house and asked her to go with me that night. We dressed up and down we went. We drove up to the bank and all was dark, but I went up and pounded on the door. Sure enough, a light came on in the bank, and a dark figure could be seen coming to the door. When he opened the door, he was all shades of red when he saw that there were two of us. After a minute's hesitation and quickly taking a deep breath he said, "Oh! I should have called you this afternoon and told you that the board had a meeting and decided to refuse your loan." Tears came to my eyes, but I walked away determined and said to my girlfriend, "I am not going to be defeated. I will take my daughter and Dad and go to Philadelphia tomorrow to the Small Business Administration." This was an agency to help small businesses like mine get started, and I had plenty of faith in the products I was making to feel confident to borrow the necessary funds to expand the business.

The figure I came up with was $72,000 that I would need for the expansion to increase my business. We got up on a sunny April day and got all gussied up, and Dad and Pat and I got in our black and white Ford Falcon and headed out for Philly. I was going to the Small Business Administration office to have an interview for getting an SBA loan.

Pat had just gotten her driver's license and wanted to drive. Off we went toward Harrisburg to get on the Pennsylvania turnpike and on to Philly. With Pat still driving, we entered the city of "Brotherly Love" and the traffic was fast, furious and the other drivers did not seem to be filled with much brotherly love. Pat soon got scared and turned down Race Street, stopped the car, and announced that she was no longer driving in this crazy city. I took over the driving. I had an address we were looking for and "sort of" directions on how to find it. (No Map Quest or GPS back then!) We more or less stumbled on the address and found a parking garage near the address of the building we were to enter. Dad had trouble walking any distance, so he said he would stay in the car and sleep or read his book while Pat and I went in to find the SBA office.

The meeting lasted several hours and, after I explained my proposed expansion and how my business operated and how it needed to grow, they said they would grant me the SBA loan for expansion of my business. I do not know if it was because I was a woman, or he liked my looks, or thought I looked honest. I had never tried for an SBA loan before, so I was very excited when they said they would grant the loan of $72,000.

We left Philly and drove to the Maryland shore. I had a meeting with a poultry broker there the next day before we headed home, so we stayed in a motel on the shore for the evening. We went to a nearby restaurant that evening, and Pat and I were going to have one drink to celebrate the achievement of my goal. Since Pat was only 16, she was not of legal age to have a drink. We were going to let Dad order a drink (teetotaler) and Pat would order coffee, and we would switch drinks when they arrived at the table and the waitress had gone away. The waitress asked Dad what he would have to drink and he said, "Missy, I don't imbibe in alcoholic beverages." I quickly kicked him under the table and I said, "He and I will each have a whiskey sour, please. She will have a cup of black coffee." Dad caught on and kept quiet.

The next morning, I met with a poultry broker, and we all went to look at a flock of chickens that I might buy for slaughter when they were mature. I agreed to buy and made the arrangements for the future delivery.

We took off for home, and we were not in familiar territory since we were in Maryland. We did manage to find the newly constructed Baltimore Beltway, which was not marked very well for strangers. It was daylight when we started our "tour" of the Beltway, and it became dark and we were still on the Beltway, going around in circles and passing the same church steeple no less than four times, each time on the opposite side of the road. Dad leaned forward from the back seat, after he had seen the same steeple for the fourth time, and said, "We have passed that same damn steeple for the fourth time." By this time, we were tired and frustrated. My daughter and I were in tears and did not know which way to go. I pulled off an exit and went to the trunk to pull out a map that I remembered I had stowed away back there. While I was examining the map, a patrol car stopped to see if we were in distress and asked if he could help us. Tearfully, we said we were lost and could he help us find our way. He said, "Where are you trying to go?" I tearfully said, "Williamsport, Pennsylvania." He said, "Oh, just go up the street about five blocks and you will come to the Susquehanna River and turn left." I almost kissed him because I would know where I was when I found the river. We did find the river, I got my bearings, and we were home in 2½ hours. It was now 2:00 a.m. in the morning, and we were tired and exhausted, but the mission was accomplished! That trip was a great success. The bank would loan me the money at 6%, and they were getting it from the SBA for 4%. I had the $72,000 in a few weeks, and I was into remodeling the processing plant to help grow my business.

After this, my typical day was like this: I would set the coffee pot to come on 15 minutes before the alarm clock rang at 5:00 a.m. When I awoke, the aroma of coffee was wafting through the air. I would get up, get dressed and go downstairs to get my first cup of coffee. I then ran out the door and down to the plant. I had a big boiler to heat a 250 gallon tank of water for scalding the chickens, and sometimes it would not turn on. So, I had to get out the 10 foot ladder and climb up and work on the electrodes that were supposed to start the boiler. I am still not sure what I did to the electrodes, but whatever it was, it worked. Once I got that going, I would go back to the house and prepare breakfast for my father. My employees started coming in at 7:00 a.m., so I had everything ready for them to begin working as they arrived. A lot of times, I had to get the truckload of chickens that were being delivered to me in off of the highway because the drivers were afraid to cross the old bridge. Many times, one of the employees did not show up, and I had to fill their shoes. We would work until 3:00 p.m. and then shut down so that the employees could clean up and have the plant ready for the next day. I would go to the house and lay down on the davenport and sleep for an hour or so and then get up, make dinner for my father and then go to the office and work until all paperwork was completed. Many days, I put in a 17 hour day with very little sleep. I think what kept my body going was all of the coffee I drank.

CHAPTER 28

Further Business Expansion

THE SBA LOAN made it possible for me to remodel the three story chicken house into a larger slaughtering plant. I had to add a "killing & bleeding tunnel." The live chickens were hung on an automated line where they hung by their feet. Their throats were cut with an electrified knife, which stunned the chickens, so they would not fling blood everywhere. The person doing this task wore heavy-duty rubber boots, gloves and an apron. The chickens went into the bleeding tunnel, and the automated line turned a corner into another room where the line dipped down into a 25 feet long, 250 gallon scalding water tank. Upon exiting the tank, the chickens went through a de-feathering machine that was a large drum with rubber fingers that rotated as the chickens passed through on their journey to the "singer," which had gas flames shooting from both sides of the chickens to take off any fine feathers. Up to this point, the chicken was still hanging by its feet. An employee had to cut the feet from the chickens and hang the chickens on another automated line. This automated line took the chickens into another room where the chickens moved over stainless steel troughs where seven employees took out the internal organs and dropped them in the trough. The eviscerated chickens continued on down the line to a washer that shot water jets from the top and both sides, and the water flowed in the opposite direction down the trough to wash the entrails into large barrels. The cleaned chickens continued down the line until they were transferred onto another automated line where they went through a "sizer." The sizer sorted the chickens by weight into four different size categories. As the chickens passed through these four weight sensors, they dropped into a large vat filled with water and ice to keep the chickens chilled. The ice water vats were chilled until they reached a designated temperature, and then they were drained, and the chickens were sent to the packing department. Each box was filled with 60 pounds of chicken and sorted by size. The chickens went into the coolers to await delivery. The chickens were sorted by weight because the retailers bought chickens based on weight according to their customer demands. There were two large walk-in coolers and ice makers that made five tons of chipped ice in 24 hours, which we used on the production line to cool the chickens after they were eviscerated.

After the business began to grow, and larger trucks were coming over the bridge to make deliveries to my business, the neighbors who lived across the road at the end of the bridge, began complaining about the rumbling noise, which was waking them up in the middle of the night. A lot of the deliveries were made very early in the mornings.

Feeling that they had a valid complaint and wanting to keep peace with my neighbors, I took my son-in-law and went to the township supervisors and asked them what could be done to eliminate the noise from the bridge. They wanted to take the cheapest way out, so in 1954, they decided to take large planks and place them at a 90 degree angle to the existing horizontal plank floor to make tracks for the trucks to drive across. This did eliminate the noise problem, and the neighbors were satisfied.

The pigs worked fine to take care of the entrails until my business began to grow even more, and then I had to find another source for the disposal of this by-product. I made inquiries and found out that a fertilizer company in Hazelton, Pennsylvania would buy them if I put them in a large barrel. They would pick them up frequently and put them in their fertilizer mix. They paid me half a cent a pound.

One day, a knock came at my front door and, when I answered the door, there stood a nice looking young man. He said, "Ma'am, would you buy a magazine from me? I have many good ones to choose from." I said, "No, I am not interested in buying a magazine." He then said, "Lady, I will do anything if you just buy one magazine." I said to him, "Well, in that case, I do have something you could do. I have a sink full of dirty dishes, and the lawn needs to be mowed." He quickly turned to go and I could not see him for the dust!

When my business was still in its infancy and my kitchen was still my office, one of the salesmen that I had talked to on the phone many times came to the door of the small building that was the plant then, and said he wanted to talk with Mrs. Warren. One of the girls that worked for me came back to the room I was working in and told me that a man was up front and wanted to talk with me. It just so happened that was the day that the young man who did the killing of the chickens did not show up for work. Any position left open was my job for the day. I had on the heavy rubber apron, which was the appropriate gear for that job. I was hanging the chickens on the moving line of shackles and slitting their necks so that they would bleed out and go into the scalder. The employee went back up front and said "Louise" will be up in a few minutes. You can imagine that I was quite a spectacle when I appeared in the front room of the plant. The salesman looked at me and said, "No, I do not want to see you. I want to see Mrs. Warren." I told him that I was Mrs. Warren. You should have seen the look on his face and he said, "You can't be Mrs. Warren because she doesn't look like that." I said, "How does she look?" He replied, "She is a short, plump lady because I have talked to her on the phone many times." Once I convinced him that I was Mrs. Warren, we stood there and discussed what he came to talk with me about concerning business.

I started having chickens shipped in by the thousands, and then it was two thousand, and soon it became apparent that I could buy them much cheaper than raising them, so now I was just in the processing business. I had a few good years at this when I was told by the assistant purchasing agent of my biggest customer that I should be prepared to lose the account. That happened when I called the buyer for his order, and he told me what he would pay me for my chickens. I told him, "No, you will not be telling me what you will pay me for my products. I will give you two weeks to get yourself established with another company." There was fierce competition from Southern plants that had taken over raising their own poultry and having their own processing plants, so now I was looking for a new source of income.

One day, my poultry supplier brought in 1,000 chickens for processing, and the young man who killed the chickens for me was sick and unable to come into work. That meant that I had to take his position on the processing line that day. The driver of the truck that brought the chickens in never offered to help unload the chicken crates full of chickens.

That left me to unload the poultry and kill the chickens while he slept in the cab of the truck. The more chickens I killed, the madder I got. The fact that I knew that my biggest customer was about to get another supplier helped me to make the decision that I had enough of this nonsense. At 3:30 p.m., the driver finally woke up and came into the plant as we were closing and asked, "Why have the crates not been put back on the truck?" He said, "Are you going to have them washed out first?" I said, "No, the crates will not be going on your truck again." He said, "Then how will I bring you more chickens?" I said, "Well, don't worry about it because you will not be bringing me any more chickens." He wanted to know what he should tell his boss. I said, "Tell your boss that you slept all day in the cab of the truck and left a woman to unload the truck by herself and kill 1,000 chickens!"

That evening, I put a sign in the office window with the message to the employees that they were not to report to work until further notice from me. I picked out a few of my long time loyal employees and told them to come into work to finish up what we had started that day and to clean the plant for shut down. The next day, I called my equipment broker in Maryland that had sold me the equipment and asked him to find a buyer for all of my equipment. It went very fast and, in about three weeks, I had an empty building.

In the meantime, I had been trying to figure out a way to sell the chicken breast meat that I was accumulating because, at that time, more chicken legs were being sold than chicken breast meat. I started experimenting with gourmet chicken breast products. This business developed slowly as I moved forward.

Three story chicken house converted to my processing plant in 1965.

CHAPTER 29

Friends, Coffee & Apple Pie

ONE DAY, EARLY in my second marriage, we were invited to a lovely dinner party put on by our neighbor, Ruth Ferree. Ruth turned out to be one of my best friends. There was also another couple there, Marty and Steve Cresswell, and they also became two of my best friends. The friendships were great and unique. We would get together every couple weeks, play cards and have a BBQ, in the summertime, out by Fishing Creek. There was a good size swimming hole in the creek up a few yards from where we had the barbecue pit. Each of the couples had two sons. They would always come along and go swimming. The two youngest sons of each couple were about my youngest daughter's age, so they were playmates. Friends would come to swim because there were not very many places where they could swim that were close to home. Ruth and Marty often went with me when I had to travel for business. We went to Detroit, New England states, Washington, DC, and many other places that I cannot recall. I was always thrilled to have their company. They went touring or shopping, while I called on my customers. Sometimes, we would be gone as long as three days, depending on how many brokers I had planned to see. Their sons were my daughter's primary playmates since we lived in the country, and they only lived a half mile from our home. Years later, my daughter told me that they would make a tent house made from a blanket hung from a tree, and they would play house. The boys decided they would be the mom or dad and all the important people of the family. But, they always made my daughter, Pat, be the family dog. Years later, one of the young men said to me, "When I see the lovely young lady that Pat has turned out to be, it makes me feel bad to think that we always made her be the dog. She always wanted to be the mother, but there was no way we were going to let her play that role."

When Ruth worked at the college as a nurse on the night shift, from 3 p.m. to 11 p.m., she would call me and ask what I was doing. Of course, I never did much anyway in the evenings because I was always too tired. She would say, "Why don't you drive down to the college, and we will play cards because this place seems to be dead tonight." It was a job that the State of Pennsylvania mandated that there be a RN available to college students and staff 24 hours a day. She was a registered nurse and a wonderful caregiver. When I was in the hospital in 1962, I had nurses around the clock. Ruth was one nurse and my older daughter, Jean, also a registered nurse, was the other one. I also had a third shift RN who just sat there in case I did need anything. When Ruth or Jean came in, no matter how bad I may have felt, I always felt better when they put their hands on me. We would just sit and talk and, maybe, I would doze off occasionally. But, they were there to take care of me. Ruth graduated from Temple University in Philadelphia, and Jean graduated from Geisinger Hospital and Nursing School in Danville, Pennsylvania. I don't know how I would have kept my sanity without these wonderful friends. When I would have a bad experience, which was many during that time, I would go down to see Ruth. She never gave me any advice. She just listened and was sympathetic. Much, much later in life, when she was very close to death, I went to visit her, and she said, "Louise, you do not know how much I worried about you during those difficult times, nor do I know how it was possible for to you to accomplish what you have today."

Steve, Marty's husband, also made that same remark to me after I had retired. He said, "I don't know how you ever did or accomplished all that you have, and I can see that Marty's and my worries were unfounded." Steve was an engineer, and when I had any machinery problems, he would come up to see if he could fix it for me.

Ruth's two boys still keep in touch, and it has not been too long ago that we visited in Pennsylvania, and two of the boys made a point to see me. What a pleasant surprise when one of them said, "I am going to take you out to lunch," and we had a lovely visit. It is so nice to hear from these young men now that they are older. They will always be young to me. They, along with Jerry Blanchard and Bill Corter, will always be very close to my heart. They were the only sons I had until I got a grandson.

There was a large oak tree near the creek in front of my house. The tree provided nice shade for the picnic table I placed there. I then built a 3 x 3 feet cinderblock bar-b-que pit on the other side of the oak tree. I would put a little kindling wood in the bottom of the pit and then place a bag of charcoal on top of the lighted kindling. It would take about 20 minutes before the charcoal was ready for cooking. My good friend's husband, George, made a rack out of wire with steel rods. The rods were about 4 feet long, and he made two halves that were about 3 feet x 2 feet. He hinged the two halves together, so the chicken pieces would be sandwiched in between the two racks. And, he left about six inches for handles on each corner, and these handles were held together with metal rings. This allowed two people to cross their arms, pick up two corners, and uncross their arms to turn the whole rack over to make sure the chicken was cooked evenly on both sides. Each time the chicken was turned, we brushed on a marinade. It consisted of one pint of water, one stick of melted butter, half a cup of apple cider vinegar, and a little salt. It may not sound very appetizing, but it sure made the chicken taste great. All of my friends looked forward to eating the chicken when it was finished. While all of this was going on, our children were having a big time in the swimming hole not far away. My girlfriends would come with food, and I also would prepare a few dishes. When their husbands were home from work, they would join us for a good meal. The children would play as we put things back in order. After that, the parents would play cards, sometimes until late at night. It often happened that the children were tired and ready for bed long before we decided to quit playing cards. We put the little ones to bed and, when we were ready to go home, we hoped that we had picked out the right children. We never made a mistake. Lots of afternoons, one of the girls would call and ask if we could go to Martin's Grove. It had a nice, large swimming hole and a small picnic area. Tables were first come, first served. So, I would say, "Since I get done at 3:30 p.m., I will take the children so that they can swim a while until our picnic supper is ready." When their husbands had finished work, they would all come, and we had fun watching our children enjoy themselves and making sure that they were safe. The children were my two girls, Joel and David Ferree, and Kit and Gregory Cresswell. Eventually, there would be many more children joining the kids in the pool of water. Sometimes, if I had time, I would make a freezer of ice cream. We had our own ice machines for my business, so getting the ice was no problem. The parents of the boys have passed away, but I am still good friends with the boys, who are now fine grown men with lovely families of their own. I am the only parent left from this group of dear friends. I am saddened each time I think of losing these wonderful friends.

There were many fun times with these dear friends. One day, I saw a recipe for an apple pie made of Ritz crackers on a Ritz cracker box. This concept fascinated me, so I decided to try it. It tasted exactly like apple pie. I went down to my friend's and told her about the pie. Her husband was there, and he had a large apple orchard. He said, "There is no way this pie would taste like real apples." It wasn't long after that, when my other good friend, Marty, was having us all for dinner and I said, "I will bring the dessert." I baked a pie with the Ritz crackers. When time came for dessert, we served the pie. The man who had the apple orchard was there. After eating the pie, he said, "Louise, that pie was delicious." I didn't say anything, but they all had a smile on their faces because they were all in on the plot to see if we could fool him. The man was not very happy with being fooled.

At some time in my life, I had decided that I did not like instant coffee. So, my girlfriends decided that they would fool me also that same night. After drinking my cup of coffee, I remarked how good the coffee was to the whole group. My girlfriend had put the instant coffee in a dripulator, so it would not look like instant coffee. When she told me what she had done, my face turned red. I was not the only one "fooled" that evening. From that time forward, I drank instant coffee, when perked coffee was not available or convenient to make. That was just one of the many good times that we shared together as friends. I was greatly grieved when each one of them passed from this world from cancer.

Dinner party at my home. My dearest friends, Ruth Ferree (right front), and Marty Cresswell (at the end of the table).

CHAPTER **30**

Aunt Edna

IN 1955, A lady we called "Aunt Edna" came to live with us. She was not really related to us, but we called her Aunt Edna because we did not want to call her Mrs. Probst. When we were children, she and her husband would come to our house every Sunday for dinner because my mother was a good cook. We always had company. Aunt Edna actually was married to the nephew of my step-grandmother. Uncle Horace was Aunt Edna's husband and, one day while out hunting, he sat down by a tree with his gun across his knee and died. Later, they began looking for him and found him there. I did not know of their financial situation, but he left her destitute. They were living in a rented house. He had cashed in his insurance policy so that he could continue tithing 10% of his income to the church.

One Sunday, I was at church and I saw Aunt Edna. I said to her, "Would you like to go up home and have lunch with me? I put a nice roast in the oven this morning, and it should be done by the time we get home." She said she would love to do that. So, she got in my car with me, and I took her home, and we had dinner, and later I took her back to her one room apartment. On the next Sunday, I saw her at church again, and I said, "Would you like to go home with me for lunch?" And, again she said she would like to go home with me for lunch. So, shortly after that when I had given my second husband the "boot," I met her at church again and asked if she wanted to come home with me for a meal. She was always willing to go home for a meal. She was living in one room without a bathroom or without water. She had to go to the bathroom to get her water, and she didn't have any conveniences at all. A bedroom was all that she could afford. She was on "relief," which we call "assistance" today. So, after about the third time of coming to meals after my husband was gone, she said, "Would you care if I stayed all night?" I told her that I would like her to stay all night. So, she stayed all night, and the next day I drove her home. The next Sunday the same thing happened. Each time she came for a meal, she stayed a little longer until, finally, after about three months, she started staying for a week at a time, and eventually it turned out to be two weeks at a time.

This worked out fine for me because I had a young child at home and often had to be away and get a babysitter. So, when she was there, my problem was solved. She and the children always got along well, so it was no problem. Eventually, she stayed as long as a month at a time. Sometimes it would only be for two weeks, depending on what mood she was in. When she stayed with us, she would wash the dinner dishes and my daughter dried them. She would always make my bed and, if I had a pair of stockings lying around, she would wash them out and, of course, she was there when the children were there.

My dad came to live with me in 1960 and she said, "I am not going to make that old man's bed," and she never did. I do not know the reason for this. But, it struck me funny that she would make that remark and she stuck to it. One of the other things she did was getting in a car with me and going with me when I had to go to different places for business. One day, we were in Williamsport, Pennsylvania, and I drove up in front of an Acme store, and she said, "Louise, I have something to tell you." And I said, "What is that?" We sat there a few moments and she reached in her pocket and came out with a little box. She said, "I noticed that you do not have a birthstone ring, and anybody who works as hard as you do should have a birthstone ring." She had taken her pitiful little amount of money and saved up enough to buy me a ring with my birthstone, which I still treasure because I know where it came from and how much she gave up to get it for me. It was a very good ring. She was the only person to ever give me a ring. Then another time, she said to me, "Louise, if I bought you a magnolia tree, would you plant it in the middle of your yard?" And I said, "Yes, I would." She said, "Take me down to the greenhouse, so I can get you a magnolia tree." So, she got me a little magnolia tree, and I planted it in the middle of my yard.

She was a lovely lady. I felt so sorry for her, but after about 10 years, in 1965, around 4:00 or 5:00 a.m., we heard a crash in the bathroom. My younger daughter was home from college, and we went over to the bathroom, and she had fainted and fell off the commode. I quickly called the doctor and covered her with a sheet until he got there. She had not regained consciousness, so they took her in the ambulance to the hospital, and she never got back home.

The child that she and her husband had taken in to raise was already married and lived away from home. In the entire 10 years that Aunt Edna lived with me, that girl had never come to see her one time. But after she died, she came out and said that her Aunt had a black onyx ring, and she wanted it. And I said, "I'm sorry, but Aunt Edna gave me the ring as a gift, and it has already been sized to my finger, and I bought a necklace and earrings to wear with it in black onyx." Long after that, I gave this ring to my younger daughter for safekeeping and to keep it in the family.

In 2011, I was back to Pennsylvania and visited the island, and that magnolia tree was still there. It was a big tree after 30 some years of growth, and the girl that currently rented the house told me that it was absolutely magnificent when it bloomed. I was so happy to see that tree was in such good shape.

Dad, me and Aunt Edna holding Tinker at Christmas, 1960.

Blooming magnolia tree that Aunt Edna gave to me. Picture taken in 1979.

CHAPTER **31**

My Mother's Stroke

ONE MORNING, IN 1957, there was a knock on my door and when I opened it, there stood my mother. It was 7:30 in the morning and I said, "Mother, how did you get here?" She said, "I came on the bus, and I'm going to have a stroke." I said, "No, Mother, you're not going to have a stroke." She said, "Yes, I am going to have a stroke." That was the day that my older daughter and her husband were moving into their new apartment. I loaded my car and put my mother in the front seat and drove into Lock Haven. Their apartment was on the third floor, and there was no elevator. We were carrying things upstairs, and by the time that I got to the third floor, a young man came running up the stairs and asked if the person was here that had the gray-haired lady in the car by the curb. He said there was a woman down there that he thought was very disturbed because she was insisting that there were rats running up under her dress. I went right down and took her home and tried to calm her down. She said, "Just let me go to bed and get back to your business." I put her in my bed and went back to help my daughter move. When I came home that evening, I fixed her dinner, and she ate and seemed to be fine. Sometime in the night, she got up and went to the bathroom. When she came back, she went to lie down on the bed and missed it completely. I didn't realize that she had a stroke, and it had blinded her left eye. I put her back in bed, and she seemed fine until the next morning. That was when I realized that she had a stroke because her left side was paralyzed. I did what I could to make her comfortable, and moved the bed up to the wall, and put a chair on the outside, and called the doctor. I brought a reclining chair upstairs so that she could see out the window and see what was going on. Every Sunday the whole family would come, plus my aunt and her family, for dinner or a barbecue. It seemed that was what made her happy. So, after about three weeks, she got up one morning and was trying to put on her stockings. I said, "Why are you putting on your stockings, Mother?" She said, "I don't know, I can't get them on, and I have to get dressed." I said, "Why do you have to get dressed?" She said, "Because I am going to go away with your sister." And I said, "No, no, Mother. You aren't going anyplace."

Well, in the meantime, my sister said she was going into town and would I cash a $40.00 check for her. I said, "Why do you need $40.00?" and she said, "Because I have to buy groceries." I said, "You know you don't have to buy groceries to stay here." She said, "Yes, I have to buy groceries." So, I cashed a check for $40.00, not realizing that she was setting me up. When she came back from town, she drove her car up in my yard right up to the front door and went upstairs and got my mother and a suitcase, which had already been packed and put in the closet, which I didn't know about. She went upstairs and helped my mother come down, put her in the car, and took my mother away. After that, she told the rest of the family that she took her because I was charging her to stay there, and she had the check to prove it. She was taking her to a trailer over in the Seven Mountain area where she was isolated from the rest of her family.

A year later, they all moved back into my mother and dad's home where we were raised and where my dad had been living by himself. But, every time there was an emergency, she would call me to come quick. "I need you." I said, "Have you called the doctor?" She said, "Yes, but the doctor said he wouldn't come." And I said to her, "Well, why not?" She said he told her that he was tired of coming because they never listened to him or did what he told them to do anyway.

I went right down and called the doctor and asked him to come. He said he was not coming. I said, "Well, my next phone call will be to the American Medical Association." That got his attention and he said, "I'll be there as soon as I can." Well, it turned out that he had to call the ambulance and take my mother to the hospital. My daughter, Jean, was a nurse at that hospital, and she wanted to go in the operating room with the doctor. He said, "No, I don't think you want to see this." My daughter insisted and was allowed to go into the O.R. Instead of the cancer that the doctors were expecting to find, they found that there was something wrapped around one of her bowels that was causing the entire problem. She was in the hospital for a while until she was back to good health.

It wasn't too long until I got another phone call saying that I'd better come because there was something the matter with Mother. I went down and looked at her, and you would have thought that somebody had jammed a watermelon into her abdomen and had left half of it sticking out. Her hernia was that bad. It was about eight or nine inches long and at least six inches across. I called the doctor again, and we took another ambulance ride to the hospital, and the doctor said it was a good thing we got there when we did because in another half an hour, it would have been too late.

In about 1959 or early 1960, they all moved to a town about 80 miles away and bought another house, again, leaving my dad alone in the family home to fend for himself.

Not long after that, my mother became ill again, and they had to bring her back to the hospital not far from where I lived. I went down every day to see my mother and one day, she said to me, "You are going to be mad at me." I said, "Well, why would I be mad at you." And she said, "Well, because I did something that you won't like." I said, "Well, what would you do that I would not like?" She said, "Well, I made a Will, giving everything to my grandchildren." That's what my mother thought, but in reality, what she had done was sign the papers that my sister had given her, which gave everything to my sister, cutting out all the rest of the family. That wasn't the only conniving thing that went on in my family because other members of my family did the same thing to my father, cutting only me out of his Will. One would think that I would have been smarter by now after having all of this happen, but I always thought that my family was honest like I would be.

My mother, in 1940, at age 57.

CHAPTER 32

Dating...Ugh!

IN THE SUMMER of 1958, you'd say that I had what might have been called a "date." I did not think of it as that because it was a man that came to have some chickens killed and, after a couple of times of doing business with me, he asked me if I would like to go to the Elk's for dinner some evening. Not getting out in male company very often, I decided to go. Everything was fine. He was a perfect gentleman but not a man that I would have picked to go out with, at least not as far as his "looks" were concerned. One afternoon, he asked if I would go for a drink. Since I had a nice experience the first time that I went out with him, I decided to go. Everything went fine. He brought me home and walked me to the door and laughed and said goodnight. He never was in my house. He would just come to the door and then leave. This went on for a while. One evening, he came to my house unannounced. He said, "Let's go out and sit by the creek." That was where I had my barbecue pit built and had a picnic table with benches. We sat on the bench and watched a beautiful scene of the creek flowing by. After a while, he put his arm on my shoulder and, a little while later, he circled my shoulders, so I could not move my arms. I didn't feel comfortable about this because I felt that he had something else in mind. Then he said, "You have been married before, so you know what this is all about." Sure enough, he began to get very aggressive. When I tried to get away, I found that he had my arms pinned tight to my body, and the only defense I had was to bite him on his shoulder. Well, it did not take him long to leave, and he never came back. Some weeks later, he had gone to a meat packing plant where I also did business. He told the owner that he was not going to ever come to the Island Poultry Farm and see that "hellcat" again. The owner asked him why, and he said that I bit his shoulder and that he would probably carry the scars to his grave. That should have taught him not to mess with me!

CHAPTER 33

B.E.N. Band Beginning

IN 1958, WHEN my younger daughter was in sixth grade, along with some other parents, we started a band and got the children instruments, and they started taking lessons, so they could integrate into the band when they went to junior high school in seventh grade. The high school (Bald Eagle Nittany HS) hired a band instructor, and these kids were the beginning of the B.E.N. Marching Band. The band was formed, but then they needed uniforms. At first, they marched in black slacks and white shirts, which were the school colors, but they really needed uniforms. So, they elected me president of the Band Association, thinking that I would be a good one to help raise the money to buy uniforms. We did everything to make money to buy the uniforms. We had bake sales, fund drives in the surrounding towns, and we decided that we could make money by having the concession stand at the football games. I furnished the lumber, and fathers of the band members got permission from the school board to build a small stand where we could sell hot dogs and sloppy joes and sodas. The band mothers would make up 10 pounds of hamburger meat into sloppy joes. We would buy hot dogs and rolls at the local A & P grocery store. This is how we earned $7,000 in several months to get black and white uniforms with hats for the band.

Everything went well for the next year. The year after that, the band director came to my office and asked me if I would be the president of the Band Association again that next year. Come to find out, he wanted me to be president again because he wanted to raise $7,000 to go to the Cherry Blossom Festival in Washington, D.C. He felt that I was the person who could successfully head that project, since I had done it the year before to get the money for the uniforms. We did everything to make money. And, I had good chicken wings that I was going to turn into fertilizer because I could not sell them. (Obviously this was way before hot wings became so popular, and I am surprised to this day that I never figured out that I could make a commercial success with chicken wings.) So, I took my barbecue grill to every festival or any place that I thought that I could sell food to families. That project turned out very well. The wings were good, and we made quite a bit of money with them. The band members also got permission from merchants in the next town to have B.E.N. tag days where they stood outside of merchants' stores and asked for donations from the passing public.

CHAPTER 34

Father Lives with Me

GOING BACK TO June 1960, I received a phone call from a neighbor of my father's. She said that she had gone to the house and found my father sitting at the kitchen table where he had sat to have his breakfast and was unable to get up. I called my son-in-law and asked him if he would go with me to get my father. Sure enough, we found him just sitting where he had been all day. We gathered up some of his belongings and took him to my home. We finally got him up the stairs and to bed. The next week, I took him to the hospital to spend two weeks being checked out to see if anything could be done to help him. He was 80 years old at this time. They were able to get him back on his feet but said that he would never be able to live alone again. I checked with my two sisters to see what they wanted me to do. They both said they would not take on that responsibility, so I took him in to live with me. Finally, he was able to get along quite well with the help of crutches. I was having a hard time financially at that time, and I asked if he would mind giving me $10.00 a week to help me out a little. He was very agreeable to that idea but never did keep his part of the bargain.

When he came to live with me, I discovered that the renters he had in his two rental houses and one apartment building were only paying him occasionally or when the spirit moved them. The renter in the best property was three years behind in his rent. Dad said he felt sorry for them so did not press for the rent. The renter was a contractor and could afford to pay the rent but did not because he realized that Dad was not going to push him for the rent. All of these issues became my responsibility. I finally did get that family out of the house after they had done a lot of damage. I sent some of my employees down to clean the place and get it in condition to rent again, and I was able to get the other tenants to get caught up on their rent. When I finally got to see his check book, I discovered that he only had a cash balance of $1,012. He had no health insurance, which at that time was not so critical since hospitals charged $25.00 a day and doctor visits were $2.00 a visit. Back then, you could still get a doctor to come to the house, if necessary, to see the patient. I did not pressure him for expense money because, after the first time mentioning it, I could see that it was not something that he was comfortable with. We got along fine and never one time in all of those years did we have an argument or disagreement. I managed to just let everything pass and kept things going as best I could.

I was able to get him $87 a month social security and about $100 a month from injury compensation from an insurance policy he had. All of the rent income I was collecting for him and interest I was paying him was put in his own bank account being saved. I took care of all his properties and sent my employees to take care of the many problems that would occur. We put on new roofs. We put in a sand mound when some of the neighbors had a dispute and cut the sewer lines, leaving the house without a sewer outlet. Then, eventually, a sewer line came through the development because the subdivision had grown quite large.

On several occasions, I was called in the middle of a cold, snowy winter night with furnace problems in one of his rentals. The furnace man would not come out unless I went to drive him. I would get up, get dressed and drive across the mountain about 14 miles to pick up this man, go fix the problems, and then drive him back home across the mountain. My dad never knew about these late night trips because I knew that it would upset him. I tried to make his life as pleasant as possible. At that time, it did not bother me that I had to do all these things for my father and many other things. He never knew I had taken care of some of the things that took place. If Dad ran out of funds, I also had to make up the shortages.

I kept my father for 16 years without a cent of compensation other than the few things that he helped me buy. All of the time, I was trying to accumulate money for him, so he would be able to leave each of his grandchildren an inheritance. He would very generously say, "Girlie, I could let you have $50.00." What I really needed was $50,000. His cash account was growing since we were getting the rents collected. Eventually, his account got up to $9,000.00.

My sister moved to Titusville, Florida, and my dad started going to Florida to spend the winters with her. I felt he could help her financially each month that he was there, and it would keep him out of the frigid cold winters of Pennsylvania and be better for his health. He did enjoy the warm weather. I insisted that he pay her $150 a month and, after much pushing, he did that. She was so hard up that I think he found out that if he did not give her monthly money that they would not eat. I went down one Christmas and found neither preparations for the holidays nor any food in the house. I bought a tree and made Christmas dinner for them and stocked the refrigerator and freezer before I came home.

As my business progressed, my typical day looked like this: A lot of times, I had to get the trucks in off the highway at 3:00 a.m. because they were afraid to come across the old bridge. (More about the bridge later.) If any of the employees did not show up for work, I had to jump in and do their job on the production line. These work days were always long, hard and tiring. I don't think anyone realized how hard I did work.

Since my dad was the only adult I had to talk to, I often spoke of needing money to keep going. When he could see that his bank account was growing, he became restless and wanted a boat. I took him to a place where they were having a sale on boats. He was expecting me to handle the boat and take him fishing. I did not have the strength or the time to help him out that way. On occasion, I would give a young man that was in my employment the day off to take my dad fishing. When they came home, the young man told me of the experiences they had and that Dad had him dragging the boat across a large field and over a railroad track to a spot where he was sure that the fishing was at its best. Needless to say, they came home empty-handed and the young man in a state of exhaustion. This young man was not willing to go fishing again. He would much prefer to stay at the plant and work. We are talking about a 9 foot row boat.

It was about this time that a flood protection dam was built about 12 miles upstream from us, and my son-in-law would take us up on weekends, and we would go for rides on the lake. Since the boat was only allowed to have four people on at a time, we took turns going. About that time, we discovered that the grandchildren were anxious to ski as many of the other families with children were doing. We soon discovered that the size motor we had was not strong enough to get a skier up out of the water. I asked Dad if he would mind if I bought a larger motor. He said that he wanted to buy the motor for his boat and that he wanted to go on the boat every time that it was taken out. That went along for a while, but the boat was too small to make for an enjoyable weekend. Things were going along for me fairly well, and I figured that if I could get a boat loan, then I could get a larger boat that all of us could ride in at one time. My son-in-law and I went to see what was available and found a boat that had been special ordered and, after the boat came to the dealer, the customer refused to buy the boat. He gave us what we thought was a fairly good deal, so now we had a larger boat. His boat and trailer was just going to be sitting there, so I asked Dad if he would like to trade his boat in toward the new larger boat. He said yes, but he wanted to ride in the front, padded swivel seat when it was used. By then, he had about $589.00 invested in the older boat and trailer. I don't remember what trade-in value he got for the boat and trailer, but the new boat that I bought was a little over $4,700. How happy and contented the children were to go to the park for a picnic and ski. All of our spare time was spent on the lake with my father always on board up front.

In 1967, my dad was reading about the World's Fair in Montreal, Quebec. He said that he had never been to a World's Fair and he would like to go. I made arrangements to take him, my youngest daughter and my nephew to the fair in Canada. We drove to Montreal, about six hours and, when we got there, we went to a hotel and discovered that there were no rooms available. The hotel had a list of citizens who would take in guests for the fair. We found a French family and stayed for two nights. Because my dad had to use crutches to walk, we were always escorted to the head of any lines at the fair. It was a good trip, and we all had a good time.

Sometime after we got back from the Canada trip, Dad read about the first night flight of a rocket launch from Cape Canaveral, which occurred in the fall. Since my sister lived close to Cape Canaveral, Florida, I made arrangements for him to fly down, so he could see the launch. I drove to Pittsburgh, so he would have a non-stop flight to Florida where my sister would pick him up.

The next fall, my best friend, Ruth, and I drove my dad to Florida. As we were going down Interstate 95, we came to a detour sign somewhere in the Carolinas. We followed the detour signs for a very long time. I thought we might be going the wrong way, so we pulled into a gas station and asked where we were.

The attendant said, "Lady, can't you read? All you need to do is follow the detour signs." I said, "Well, it seemed like we were going east a long time and I thought we should be going south." He said, "Well, if I was going to Florida, which I ain't, this is the road that I would take." I could see that he was disappointed because I was not a gas customer, so I filled up with gas. We kept on going, and we finally reached my sister's home about 11:00 at night. We stayed overnight and the next day we started back to Pennsylvania. As we were coming up Interstate 75, we came to Interstate 475, which was the beltway around Macon, Georgia. After traveling down this road for about two miles, the car just "died!" I was able to pull off to the side of the road. I belonged to the AAA and, when I had joined the last time, they had given me a large piece of paper with instructions on one side and in big letters "HELP" on the other side. It was getting dusk, and we were not sure what to do. I remembered I had that paper from the AAA. I got it out of the trunk and held it up to the window of my car. A pickup truck stopped to try and help us. He and his wife were very helpful. He said he had some type of cell phone, but he was out of range. He drove several miles back to get in range and called a garage for assistance.

When he came back, he said that it would be a while before a tow truck would be out to get us. He and his wife came back and said that they were on their way to a fish fry when they had stopped to help us. They asked us if we wanted to go along. Neither Ruth nor I was interested in a fish fry, so we waited for the tow truck. Eventually, it pulled up beside us and towed us back into Macon. The garage was in a rather remote looking site. The tow truck driver left and told us that there would be someone along to help us. We sat in the car and saw a big police dog pacing around our car. We started to get scared, and we decided that we should hide our money. We decided to put it in our bras. A man finally came and told us what was the matter with the car, but he wasn't sure that he would be able to get the part for it that evening. We were really in a panic, but after a while, he came back and said, "You are in luck. I found the part."

He worked on the car for a while and then said, "There you are, ladies. Try and start the car." I started the car and it turned over. I said to the man, "How much do I owe you?" He said, "$46.00." I said, "OK, I will write you a check." He said, "No, I will not take a check. It has to be cash." So, Ruth and I looked at each other and said, "Now what do we do?" Since we had hidden the money in our bras, we didn't want to fish the money out while he was standing there looking at us. We decided to turn toward each other and get the money out of our bras. He was a very nice man, and he told us not to stay in a hotel in that area and to hold on to our pocketbooks. We told him we were not sure how to get out of that area and back on the interstate toward home. He said, "Just follow me and I will get you out to the highway." We found a hotel along the interstate for the night. The rest of our trip back to Pennsylvania was uneventful.

I did not realize at the time that my father was telling family members that he bought the new boat and that it was his boat. They believed him and that was a strike against me. The same thing happened with the car. I had a little Ford Falcon and was traveling from the Catskills every week to work, taking my father with me. After a couple of trips, he informed me that the car was too uncomfortable for him and that I should get a bigger car. At that time, I could not take on any more large debts, nor did I have the money for a down payment. He said, "I have $500 to put toward it," so I agreed to start looking and find out what I could do. I found a blue Oldsmobile that was heavy and very comfortable. Well, he was delighted and again he sat in the front seat almost every time the car moved, even if it was just to go to the post office. I discovered later that the family was led to believe that he bought me the car. Strike two against me. It was a few years later that I discovered that he told the family that he owned the Island Poultry Farm, which was my business. I thought that if it made him happy to think that he owned the place, what difference did it make? That was a big mistake because the family believed that also. That was strike three against me! I guess they thought I was pretty dumb to put all of my money and energies into something that was not mine.

For years, my dad had not seen my mother. One morning in 1965, my father went on my delivery truck to Jersey Shore, Pennsylvania on some kind of business and, when he came back, the family had gathered at my house. When my dad came in he said, "What a surprise." My brother just blurted out, "Mother is dead." I had not planned on giving him that message in that manner. I said to my brother, "Why did you do that?" He said, "Well, that's the way they came to me when I was on the bulldozer and told me that I was to come here to your house because my mother had died."

After Mother died, Dad said, "Girly, I am going to put everything in your name." I said, "Dad, please don't do that because you know the stink that would make." He said he felt that would make things much better, and he knew that I would follow his wishes, but I protested.

I said, "They are not good to you now, so think how much worse it will be if you do that." Dad went down to make a Will and left the homestead to my one sister. My brother was to get the large apartment building. And since my other sister had gotten the whole farm and all the money that my mother had, he did not leave her anything in his Will. He had a small house on one of the lots in the development and that was to be mine and the few acres of undeveloped land that he had.

My father in back and his sisters.
L to R: Aunt Helen and Aunt Bertha in 1971.

Dad with his "big catch" in 1972.

CHAPTER 35

Row, Row, Row Your Boat

IN 1964, THE water was rising on the creek banks on both sides of the island from extensive storms we were having.

Jerry Blanchard worked for me during high school and after he returned from military service. I asked Jerry to bring in my dad's row boat before the banks overflowed and tie it up to a tree near the house.

In several days, when the water was starting to recede, I asked Jerry to take Dad's boat back out to the creek bank. Jerry saw that the shortest way to the creek bank was now dry, and he would have to drag the boat about 200 or so feet to get it to the creek bank that was in the front of my house. The field in back of my house was still filled with water, so he thought he would drag the boat the shorter distance to the water and then pull it up to the top end of the island in the water. He put on tall waders to stay dry while he pulled the boat up the field in the water. The water in the field was not raging like the water in the stream was still raging. He got to the top of the field and hopped into the boat, ready to row with the oars as the boat hit the raging stream water. The boat immediately flipped over on top of him. He was pulled under the violent, rushing water, and his waders quickly filled up with water, and he was being dragged down under the churning water as he was being pulled downstream.

He was swept downstream, and he kept grabbing for anything he could hold on to near the bank, but every time he caught hold of something, it broke away. He was continually being forced underwater due to the heavy water-filled waders. He was in the raging stream for quite some time, desperately grasping for anything that would stop his further descent downstream and enable him to crawl out of the water. He does not remember how long this all took (a lifetime to him), but when he neared the bridge that provided the only way onto the island, which was in front of my house, he finally caught hold of a tree root or something that did not break off. By this time, he had swallowed a lot of muddy water and also had muddy water in his lungs. He crawled, exhausted, out of the raging water and started his slow, slow crawl on hands and knees to the house. I did not know when he had gone out, so I was not thinking about where he was or how long he might be taking. I also did not realize he would decide to brave the raging waters to get my dad's boat back to the river bank where the waters had receded.

He reached the house and could not get up the front door steps. He grabbed a handful of dirt and started throwing it up the several steps to the front door because he did not have the energy or strength to crawl up the steps. My daughter happened to be in the living room and heard what she thought was a neighbor's cat scratching at the front screen door. She ignored the noise at first, but it persisted, and she finally went to the door to see what was making the noise. To her complete and utter surprise, there laid Jerry at the bottom of the steps, and he could barely speak. She could see that he had been in the water, even though the flood waters were not near the front of the house at this point. She yelled for me to come quick and, when I saw the situation, I immediately called the doctor (they would still come to the house in our sleepy little town) and Jerry's parents. My daughter dragged him into the living room and rolled him on to his stomach. She had been taught in school that she should put his arms above his head and bend his elbows, and then push upward on the mid-upper back, and then raise the folded elbows to help force the water out. Lots of brown, muddy water came rolling out of his mouth, and she continued the back compressions and elbow lifts until no more water was coming out of his mouth.

The doctor arrived as quickly as possible, and we had Jerry on the sofa by that time. The doctor listened to his lungs and said that there was water in them and that he would be OK, but he would have to rest for a few days until he was feeling better. I do not remember if he was given any medication by the doctor, but he did slowly recover over the following weeks.

Needless to say, he had learned a healthy respect for the power of a raging stream, but he never let it stop him from safely enjoying water sports and recreation throughout his lifetime. "Safely" being the operative word. He was in the same class as my daughter and his future wife. They all graduated from high school, Jerry went to the Army and, when he came back, he got married to his high school sweetheart. He came to me to ask if he could put their trailer on the island. He came to work for me and stayed for four years. He was a wonderful employee and friend. We still communicate often and visit yearly. When he worked for me, he always called me "Boss." He still calls me "Boss" to this day!!

Jerry Blanchard, owner of Miller's Furniture of Mill Hall.
Photo taken in 2014.

CHAPTER 36

The "Catskills" New York

AFTER I STOPPED the poultry slaughtering business, I only had a bookkeeper and a few ladies working for me while I worked on expanding my gourmet chicken product line. Things were still rather tight financially. I was desperate at this time because I was afraid that I would lose my business. Fortunately, out of the blue, I got a phone call from the owner of a kosher poultry plant in the Catskills, New York to come and work with them for a while to get their production back on track. I saw an opportunity to pick up some easy cash and at $250.00 a week and an apartment to live in. I could not pass this up. I only had to work Monday, Tuesday and Wednesday and then was able to come back home and take care of my own business. My dad was living with me at that time, so I packed him up, and we were off on a new adventure.

I was only there a few days until one of the employees came to me and said, "We all know that he brought you up here to show us how to get this line going and how to debone chicken breasts, and then he is going to let you go." I thanked her and told her not to worry because I knew how to take care of myself.

When we first talked about our business arrangement, he said that he wanted to make me a partner and all of these wonderful benefits I was to get. Well, I knew then that something was not right because no one gives half of anything away just for a little consulting work.

Not long after I was there, I could see that he did not need help with his slaughtering process because it was going about the way he wanted it to. It was a kosher operation but, when the Rabbis were paid to turn their heads, the plant was run the same as any other plant. He had his office rigged up so that bells started ringing and the ice machines and cold water started when an inspector came in because, in a kosher plant, everything has to be done with cold water. Otherwise, hot water was used for production processes. On the days the owner knew the inspectors were visiting, everything was run as a kosher operation. If the inspectors came unexpectedly, he had a bell installed under his desk, and he would press the bell with his foot, and the plant immediately went into a kosher operation.

About ten weeks into this job, there was a heavy ice storm, and I walked down from my apartment to the plant to tell them to put salt on the sidewalks, so the employees would not fall when they were leaving work. Wouldn't you know, I fell on the ice and broke my wrist! I was taken to the hospital, and the owner's wife thought my accident was the funniest thing, and she just laughed and laughed. I never did understand her reaction.

I stayed out of work for a week. The owner told me that he would not need my services any more, and I told him that was OK. I hired a driver to go pick up my younger daughter, who was in Hazelton, Pennsylvania at her college roommate's house. Hazleton was not far from where I was in New York, and Pat drove us back home.

While I was working at the kosher plant, I had received a call from my bookkeeper saying that the Island Poultry Farm account was over-drawn. This was the second time this had happened, and I did not understand how it was happening when the deposits had been made on time. This was at the same bank that would not loan me the money. I took my dad and went home, and we went to the bank and my dad guaranteed a note for $1,500.00. Shortly after that, the bookkeeper discovered what was happening. We were not getting credit for our deposits. I went to the banker and showed him where we had made the deposits and had not been given credit. He turned and went in the back and came right back out and said,

"You are right. The hardware store's name starts with an "I" and we accidently put it in his account instead of your business account." When this had happened the first time, I had adjusted my books and gave up on finding what I thought must have been my mistake. Since this happened, I decided to go back six to eight months to when we had been short before and found that there were deposits for which we had not been given credit. He called the hardware man and told him what was going on, and the hardware store owner said he never checked his accounts because he figured the bank was always right. What a bunch of bull that was!

In August, I got a call from the New York State Employment Disability Compensation Insurance Department. They wanted me to come up to New York to talk about my accident when I slipped on the ice while working up there. I took my dad and we went to New York. When I went to the department, I told them who I was and was told to sit down and wait for someone to come and talk with me.

In a little while, a man called me back and said, "I understand that you broke your wrist while you were working at this plant." I said, "Yes, I did." He asked me how it was and I said, "Oh, it is OK." He asked to see my wrist and he said, "Your wrist does not look quite straight." I said, "No, it isn't, but it is OK." He said, "Go back out and sit down in the other room, and I will be with you shortly."

He called me back in and asked, "Would you sign a release form for $1,800?" I couldn't grab that pen fast enough! I had been getting worker's compensation all of that time, and they were giving me a final settlement of an additional $1,800. They said I would get the check by Christmas and, indeed, I did. I was making some money in my plant, but not a lot, so this $1,800 really helped me.

At this time, I was only making interest payments to the bank on my loan, but they never said anything to me about it. When I could finally get caught up, I started paying my full principal and interest payments again. That was how I got by with hard work and by doing the right thing by everyone who helped me along the way. I always tried to be very careful with my money.

CHAPTER 37

My First Chicken Patty

I APPLIED FOR my second SBA loan and remodeled the three story chicken house again. I turned it into a frozen food processing plant. I was still experimenting with different frozen chicken recipes at that time. I discovered that I was having a lot of white meat portion control medallions that had to end up in some kind of a product, but I was not sure what. I ground it and made little meat loaves, and took my little hamburger patty maker from my kitchen and formed patties and discovered that they were delicious when fried and put on a hamburger bun. I worked on this idea for quite a while and soon discovered that there was a market for them, and that my little hand-held hamburger-maker was not going to make enough product to meet the demand.

I called the Hollomatic Company because I knew they had a machine used to press out hamburgers. The salesman was very emphatic about the machine not being able to press out ground chicken meat. I said, "Send me your cheapest machine, and I will make it work." I know the salesman thought I had "lost it," but I was determined because I had been working with this chicken product for some time. I had a good idea how it had to be done to make it work. Well, it did work and that was the beginning of my chicken patty product. At first, I called it chicken steak, but when the government said that I could not call it that because the meat was ground, I had to change the product name to "chicken patty."

After experimenting with the chicken, I discovered that keeping the chicken meat at 40 degrees would allow the patty to form perfectly as it came out of the hamburger patty machine. If the temperature was above 40 degrees, the patties were too sticky to handle in order to hand bread them. If the temperature was lower than 40 degrees, a chunk would fall out of the patty as it exited the patty machine. The machine had an inner lever that automatically put a sheet of waxed paper between each patty as it exited the machine. When six patties were in a stack, they were put on a cookie sheet and placed in a freezer until they were stiff enough to be brought out and hand battered. We used a roaster pan filled with a batter mixture that I formulated and placed six patties on the handled rack and dipped them down into the batter. When the rack was raised, each patty was hand breaded and 12 patties were placed in a shipping box and put back in the freezer.

The demand for this product became so great that I realized that making these patties 12 at a time by hand would not work to meet the demand of my sales. One of my largest single accounts was a nearby university. They used them in their cafeteria, and the chicken sandwich was a big hit with the 29,000 students at that time. I also had brokers in multiple states selling this product to distributers, who then sold to restaurants and other end-users.

Now, I am faced with coming up with a new idea for making the patties in larger amounts more efficiently. I heard about this company in Sandusky, Ohio that made commercial breading machines. I called them and, after talking with a salesman, I determined that they may have what I needed, but I wanted to go see it before I committed to buying it.

I called my son-in-law, who was taking flying lessons, and I asked him if he and his instructor would fly me to Sandusky, Ohio to see this equipment. He said to me, "I thought you were afraid to fly in a small plane." I said, "Well, I have to do what I have to do!" So, off we flew the next week to Sandusky.

I ordered the machine, and it was delivered the next week. It had a conveyor belt and, when the patty came out of the patty maker, it dropped onto the conveyor belt and was taken through a trough, which held my batter mixture. As it traveled along, it came out of the batter and went through the breading machine, which coated the patty on top and bottom. As the patties came out of the breading machine, they were to be boxed 12 in a box and then put in the freezer.

One problem I did not foresee was that the machine was plopping out patties faster than one person could put them in a box. I found this out on the trial run with the machine. I was standing at the end of the line, trying to keep up with the patties coming out and, as I got behind, the patties began falling on the floor. Tears started to run down my cheeks and I yelled, "Stop the machine! This is not going to work." (I felt like Lucille Ball in her episode in the candy factory with the conveyor belt of chocolates.) Not to be deterred, I thought about it for a few minutes and decided to try two employees on either side of the conveyor belt, who grabbed every other patty and put 12 of them in a box. This worked better, but neither person had time to take the box away because the patties kept right on coming. So, I had to have a third person to take the boxes away and replace them with an empty box for each person, so the line could keep moving. This solved my problem with increasing production for this particular product.

Then another problem arose. The customers wanted the patties to be pre-browned so all they had to do was heat them up. So, back I flew to Sandusky, Ohio to look at a commercial frying machine. This machine was about a foot wide and eight feet long and about eight inches deep. I had to put about 5 inches of oil in this trough, and the conveyor belt would carry the patties down through the hot oil, and they would come out pre-browned and ready to box. After this, we only made this style patty because "TV Dinners" were becoming popular, and people wanted a product that required less preparation and still tasted good. My chicken patty met this requirement.

Yet, another problem arose. I discovered that I could no longer make the quantity of batter to meet the demands of the product. I had to try and find a company that made a batter that was similar to the batter I had formulated. I also had to find a company that made a breading that tasted like the one that I was making. I found these companies by trial tasting their products, and they were able to supply me with all of these products in large quantities. I started buying these products several hundred pounds at a time and, eventually, was ordering a ton at a time.

Ultimately, buying this much breading was the main factor that led to the sale of my business. More about that later.

CHAPTER **38**

My Employees

GOING BACK TO mid-1946, I had two daughters, the youngest just a baby, my other daughter about 11 years old, and the beginning of a business.

It was after this that the chicken business really got started. It started out slowly with only women as employees. The first two ladies that I had working for me were older ladies. As a matter of fact, they were grandmothers. They worked very hard but, one day, when I came into the plant, they were in a heated argument about religion. I didn't know quite what to say, so I said, "It is our policy here to never discuss religion or politics." That way, I thought it would avoid trouble later on when I began to grow and advertise for employees. I had lots of applicants. Among them were two ladies that were a little on the heavy side, but I decided to hire them. They told me that they had been looking for work for three years, and that nobody would hire them and how glad they were that they found a job. They were good workers and were employed by me for 25 years each. I thought they were always happy working for me. One of them always acted like she was happy working for me to my face, but when she thought that I was out of hearing distance, I heard differently. One day, I had to leave the plant for a while, and I let the employees know what had to be done in my absence. As I was walking out the hallway, I heard her say to the other employees, "Why didn't you tell the son of a bitch to do it herself?" I turned around and said to her, "Come to my office." She came and I said, "How many years were you trying to get a job and I was the only one that gave you the opportunity to work?" She said, "Three years," and I said to her, "The next time you want to call me an S.O.B., don't let me hear you. I will let it go this time, but the next time, I will be showing you the exit door!" I don't know whether she ever said that again or not, but she was one of my very best workers and was with me until I sold the island and business in 1980.

In 1963, a young lady came in for a job application. After reading it, I decided that she would fit into our program very nicely. She was a very good worker and could do anything, including fixing minor things on the truck and refrigeration units. She was there about three years, when her husband came in and asked me to fire her. I said, "No." She was one of my best workers and her husband was not the one that asked for the job. He was very angry and left. It was shortly after that they were divorced. That left her with three children to take care of. She lived in a trailer up in the mountains. It seemed that she did not have the money to pay for water and rent, so being as handy as she was, she dug into the water main and brought water into her trailer. This went on for several years before it was discovered. She came to work one morning and told me what had happened. She was without water. I had no way of helping her in that situation so I said, "Would you like to have a new trailer in the trailer park." She did not have the money to do that, so I told her that I would buy the trailer, and she could pay me a little bit each pay day. She seemed pleased, and the other employees in the plant took up donations to buy her the necessary things such as the linens, dishes and what have you. I thought she was in pretty good shape.

About 1968 and 1969, I would come in from work exhausted and lay down on the davenport for a few hours of rest before going out to mow the acreage. I would get awake, and there she and her children would be sitting watching me. I didn't think too much of this, but my oldest daughter kept insisting that she was a lesbian. In about six weeks, I discovered that she had a girlfriend. I did not know this at first, but after going to my house during break and at noon, my phone was always busy and that was the time when I took care of a lot of my business by phone, and I only had one line. One afternoon, I asked the manager of my plant if she knew who was on the phone every time I went to use it. She said, "Don't you know?" and I said, "No, why?" and she told me that it was my employee calling her girlfriend. I could not believe that. So I asked her, and she said it was her. I told her it would have to stop. After that, she started going home at lunchtime.

She only lived with this lady for about six months when they decided to move to another more isolated area in a trailer. It was not long after that when she decided to quit working for me and went to work at a gas station. She had already left the trailer and her children and went to live with the other woman. Her husband came and took the children and left the trailer empty.

We heard that one of the ladies began cheating on the other and that caused a big fight. It so happened that the end of that was very tragic. Her girlfriend threw a knife at her as she was leaving the trailer one day, and it hit her in the back and went through her heart. She died instantly, as I understand it. The girl got a 10 year prison term. I do not know what has become of those children after all these years.

Now, I had a trailer on my hands. I put an ad in the paper "trailer for rent." I told my son-in-law, who was working for me at that time, that he should go and interview the prospects that wanted to rent. When he came back, he said, "The trailer is rented, but you will not be very happy." I said, "Why is that?" He told me that he had rented to a black family. I said, "That's all right as long as they pay the rent." They rented for about a month, and the lady that was renting came to see me. She told me that she was sorry, but her husband had been put in prison for selling drugs. I felt so bad for this young lady. She was so nice and had a darling little girl. She stayed there for a while and would often come to my house for a meal, and I would give her chicken products and produce from my garden. I know that this was probably more food than she had and this went on for some time. One day, she came and said, "I will have to move and you will have to go to the prison and get my husband to sign off on the rental agreement." We went, and that was my first experience in going to a federal prison and I hope my last. So, now that he had signed the papers, I was again a trailer owner. I put another ad in the local paper "trailer for sale," and, eventually, a young married couple bought it and moved it on a trailer lot of their own.

I am happy to say the young lady whose husband went to prison had a happy ending. She found me when I was in my nineties and called me. I was very surprised when I got the message and called her back. She said that her husband had been rehabilitated in prison and, when he got out, he became a minister and that they had nine children. She told me that I had made a life-changing time in her life, when I had been kind to her and helped her when her husband was in prison.

About 1963, Jerry Blanchard came to work for me in his junior year of high school. He did all the little chores that were getting to be too much for me. He planted flowers, made a path of field stone from the patio to the front of the house, put up my Christmas tree and my lights outside, and many other little jobs that I could find for him. He did this work for me for a good many years, finally ending up driving the truck, loading and unloading trucks, and helping my maintenance man, Dick Falls. Dick chewed tobacco, which was fairly common for working men to do in the farm country where we lived. I never could tell that he was chewing, but I saw the shape of the can in his back pocket. One day, Jerry saw him chewing snuff and said, "I'd like to try some of that chewing tobacco." Dick chuckled and gave him a big wad of Skoal chewing tobacco. Jerry tells me all of these years later, that in about 15 minutes after he started chewing the tobacco, he got really sick and probably turned "green." Dick was laughing the whole time. Jerry asked Dick, "How do you chew that stuff?" and Dick said, "Well it takes practice, and it is pretty rough the first time you try it, especially with a big wad." Jerry said that cured him of ever wanting to chew tobacco again. Since Dick was a very nice man, I think there may have been a "method to his madness" in giving Jerry a big wad, so he would not get started with a bad habit. Jerry was with me for a long time and finally went out on his own sometime after the 1972 flood. Jerry was another of these young men that I felt was more like a son than an employee. Jerry and his wife Sandy are still among my good friends, and we try to see each other at least one time a year and talk often on the phone.

Dick's wife also worked for me, and they were both great employees. I had a few employees that I could always count on who worked for me for a long time. At the peak of my business, I had 81 employees. Some employees came and left, and I figured they were probably better off at some other job anyway.

Of course, I did not know at this time how far this enterprise was to go. I would put my baby up on the shelf I had made where she would be warm and dry, and I would work sometimes way into the night after the ladies would go home. This operation was manned by women until only a few years before I sold in 1980. For a number of years, I employed only one man, and the rest of my employees were women. As my business grew, and I needed stronger muscles to load and unload trucks and also a truck driver to handle the established routes for delivering products from Pennsylvania all through the New England states, I hired more employees and more of them were men. We had regular runs to Pittsburgh and Philadelphia and stops in between.

I hired a nephew, by marriage, to drive a truck for me. One day, he was making the New England run. I told him that he could not take any of his young children with him because the truck was not covered with insurance to cover passengers riding in the truck. He had gone onto a street that had a low overpass and, when he tried to drive under it, the impact took off the top two feet of my refrigerated truck. He called me to report the accident and told me that he had his little boy with him. Neither of them was hurt, thank goodness. I told him to rent a car to get back home because the truck was completely disabled and could not be driven. When he got back, I asked him why he took his young son with him when I had already told him he could not take passengers. He said, "Well, he wanted to go." That was the last of him because I had to let him go. Sometime later, a man sent me a picture of the damaged truck, and he said that I would not believe that there was no one hurt in the accident. After seeing the picture, I agreed.

Many of the distributors sent their own trucks to pick up product. The sales were mostly generated by the broker that had taken on my line of products.

I was very fortunate that most of my employees were the best that anyone could ever hope for. The female employees were hard working and loyal to a fault. I can never say enough good things about my loyal employees. Many of them were doing jobs that would be a challenge to many men. I am sure that these ladies did not realize how much I valued their loyalty and considered each and every one as my friend.

I also had a lovely lady, Helen White, who came once a week and cleaned my house, did laundry and ironing. She knew more about my house than I did and took care of it as if it was her own. She is a dear friend, and we still stay in touch and I love her like a sister. She was always better to me than my own sisters. I have gifts from her that go with me everywhere I move, and I am constantly reminded of this kind and considerate person.

Refrigerated truck after hitting the overpass.

My dear friend, Helen White, in 2014.

CHAPTER 39

My First Food Broker

I WAS STILL experimenting with recipes for gourmet chicken products and was selling it along with my fresh poultry that I was buying and reselling at that time. A food broker came across these products and came knocking on my door to see if he could represent me as a sales force. This was a life-changing day for me and my business. Until that day, I did not know what a "food broker" was or did. He explained to me that he had gotten some of my products and thought that I needed his help in promoting the sales. He told me what a broker's functions were and that it was like a "marriage." Well, being familiar with that word, I became a little suspicious of what I was getting into, but needing a sales force of some sort, I gave it a try.

He wanted me to sign papers stating that he would get "half a percent" of all my earnings for the rest of my business life. The killing word was the "marriage" one. From experience, I knew that I did not want anything to do with that event again. This went on for about a year and then I went to his office about 80 miles away for a meeting. He wanted the papers signed then. When I refused to sign this agreement, he took me in to see his son and told me that he would no longer represent me. His son said, "I will represent her because we are making too much money from her account not to represent her." I honestly think that it was a contrived deal, (good cop, bad cop routine), but any way, things went smoothly after that.

His son and family were wonderful to me, and I think a lot of them to this day.

Then came the day when I needed to have the government's USDA approval so that I could sell across state lines with my products. The broker told me that there was a poultry convention in Atlanta and that I should go. Of course, I did not have the money, so he said that he would pay and add it on to my existing bill. The existing bill was originally started in the beginning of our business relationship when I did not have the money to pay his company's commissions on what was sold. He agreed to put it on an account, which I could pay back when my cash flow became positive.

The head of the inspection division for the USDA would be at this convention, and my broker said he would get me in contact with him while we were there. We had the meeting, and the inspector told me that if he could see the blue prints of my facility, he would be able to help me. I said I just happen to have them with me. After looking at them, he said that I needed a loading dock with a drain and that I should not write any more, but call instead, and ask for him directly. I went home and put in a small concrete slab with what looked like a drain, only I knew the drain was for show and did not go anyplace.

When I was struggling to get the business going, I seemed to be having one setback after another. I read an ad in the paper for an inspector and you had to take a civil service exam. It was held at Williamsport High School, about 34 miles away. I decided to take the test in case I was unable to get this business going enough to educate my children and keep the roof over our heads. I thought this could be a way to have another income if I did not get the USDA approval I needed to grow my business. To my amazement, I passed the test, and they called me to take a position.

About this same time, I was notified that my federal inspection approval had come through, so now I had a conflict of interest. I called the number provided in the notification and explained my situation. The man I spoke with said he was glad that it had worked out for me, but they were disappointed that I could not take a position at that time. The man I spoke with said, "I am sorry that you cannot take a position, but if it doesn't work out for you, here is a number for you to call me back, and I will find a job for you." Well, that was reassuring, because I still wasn't sure that things were going to go in my favor.

He told me that of the 27 people taking the test that I was their top choice. I only had a high school education, so I thought that maybe I was not as dumb as my family had always led me to believe.

After getting the USDA inspection approval, this meant that an inspector had to be assigned to my plant to see that everything was clean, sanitary and that the poultry was properly handled to prevent persons from getting sick from eating it. Since there was not anybody qualified to take this position, a local veterinarian, whose wife and I were very good friends, took on the job just to help me out.

So, now I am able to sell any place in the U.S. or around the world, with an identification of P-756 under the product name of Mrs. Warren's Poultry Products Mfg. by Island Poultry Farm Inc., P.O. Box 192, Mill Hall, Pennsylvania 17751. What a victory!!

Every box of product had to have a label or a sticker on it identifying the product with the appropriate count, size and ingredients. I also had an in-house secret code that was stamped on every box so that we knew what day the product was produced and could tell when it had left our plant.

After that, I was able to sell any place and did so with appointed brokers in other states. Occasionally, I would travel to Detroit, Philadelphia, Pittsburgh, Jacksonville, the New England states, and New York City to assist brokers in promoting my chicken products as they called on their customers. I also did many food shows. I was a one woman show as far as product development, ordering all supplies needed to make products, marketing, sales, and supervising the production plant. One of my employees gave me a plaque that hung on my office wall that said, "I may not always be right, but I am always the Boss!"

When we made the trip to Atlanta to go to the convention and meet with the USDA, the broker said, "If we get one room, it will be less expensive." I told him I might be poor, but not that poor and that I would not consider anything but having my own room. He was visibly upset, but that was alright with me. I went to Atlanta in a 3-engine prop plane but came back on what was my first jet plane ride.

My broker came one day and told me that to successfully get things going that I had better plan to attend food shows. He said there was one that was being held in Harrisburg and that we would go and cook products for potential customers. I did not have any equipment for doing this, but he assured me that he had everything necessary if I would just furnish the products.

Well, this was an education that I had not counted on, but what an experience. It turned out to be more than one day, so I had to go out and buy some clothes because I had only taken enough for one day. After a couple of days on my feet cooking and talking, I was exhausted but pleased with the outcome. The next day after coming home, the president of the Motel Association called and invited me to do a cook-off in the Poconos at one of their meetings. I had never been there before, so again, I did not know what I was getting into. The man said that they never had food demos at their conventions but that a number of folks had been by my booth at the food show in Harrisburg and were so impressed with my products that they decided to invite me to attend. I did not have what I felt were the right clothes, so one of my employees said that she had a fur piece that looked like mink, but it really was rabbit. I took a basic black dress that my daughter had given me for Christmas. What an experience. I drove and drove, thinking that this place must be the end of the earth, but eventually I arrived and was treated like royalty. People pitched in and helped to set up my booth. In the evenings, I was invited to attend all of their social functions, which were quite elaborate and certainly a very new experience for me. The night that they had their dinner dance, I wore the black dress with a gold belt and gold necklace and earrings and the fake mink stole. When I walked into the convention center, an eerie hush came over the crowd, and people started to come up to me and one lady grabbed my arm and said, "You are my guest for the evening and will be sitting at my table." She owned a motel outside of Pittsburgh, and we remained friends until she passed away some years later. We visited each other often, and we visited Hawaii together. Those three days passed quickly, but I made some great and lasting friendships. This was the very beginning of many, many food shows all over the country.

UNITED STATES CIVIL SERVICE COMMISSION

NOTICE OF RATING

APPLICANT MUST FILL IN ALL BLANKS DOWN TO HEAVY BLACK LINE

EXACT TITLE OF EXAMINATION

DATE OF EXAMINATION

POULTRY INSPECTOR

NAME MARGARET Louise K WARREN

ADDRESS RD #1 Box 42

CITY AND STATE Mill dall, Pa 1775'

This is not a notice of appointment. It is a record of your rating. It is important that you keep it. It is noted that your application was not rated for any position with a lower entrance salary than that which you indicated thereon.

Your Rating is — ELIGIBLE

☐ This examination is not rated on a numerical basis

☒ Your numerical rating is: 87.2, GS-5

Your Rating is — INELIGIBLE for the reasons checked below:

☐ The lowest acceptable salary indicated on your application is higher than the salary shown on our announcement.

☐ You did not pass the written test. All competitors must attain an earned rating of 70 without regard to veteran preference. When an applicant's paper falls below the passing mark it is not scored further. Ineligibles do not receive a numerical grade.

☐ Your application does not show that you meet the minimum requirements as to experience (or education) which were specified in the examination announcement.

☐ Your eligibility is suspended pending your furnishing the Commission proof of correction of physical condition, as shown on the attached notice.

☐ Failed to reply to official correspondence.

☐

IF THERE IS A CHECK BELOW, IT INDICATES THE AMOUNT OF VETERAN PREFERENCE CREDIT INCLUDED IN YOUR RATING

☐ 5 POINTS—IF YOU ARE APPOINTED YOU WILL BE REQUIRED TO FURNISH TO THE APPOINTING OFFICER EVIDENCE OF HONORABLE SEPARATION FROM THE ARMED FORCES.

☐ 10 POINTS

If you have received an eligible rating, be sure to read the important message on the back of this form.

Executive Secretary
Board of U. S. Civil Service Examiners
Eastern Area Administrative Division, C&MS
U. S. Department of Agriculture
Room 742-A, Federal Center Building
Hyattsville, Maryland 20781

JUN 9 1965

(Issuing Office and Date of Issue)

CSC FORM 4008
SEPTEMBER 1962

CHAPTER 40

Gourmet Chicken Products

SO FAR, I have raised chickens from day old "peeps," as baby chicks are often called, an experience that turned into a disaster, and I am stuck with them. I turned that around and was in the business of producing eggs. Then, came the necessity of getting rid of the non-producers, so now I am in the slaughtering business. This went on for a number of years and continued to grow until I found myself in a position of having sold more chicken legs in proportion to breasts or white meat. Now, I had to figure out a way to get rid of the excess white chicken meat. Finally, I got the idea of filling the breast meat with bread filling that my mother always used to fill her chickens. Some called it dressing, but we called it "filling." I kept experimenting with different chicken white meat products while I was still slaughtering poultry to have an income. Big national food companies started doing these kinds of products, but I was doing them before these companies started doing their products. This product caught on well, and the demand became greater and greater, especially after I had created a sales force of nine brokers in as many states. I stopped slaughtering and turned my plant into a full-time gourmet chicken production plant. As I was making this transition, I was still experimenting with adding new products to my line of gourmet chicken products. I ended up formulating the following products from white meat of chicken: Chicken Cordon Bleu, Chicken

Hawaiian, Chicken Kiev, Pennsylvania Dutch Filled Chicken Breasts, Chicken A La Continental Supreme, Breaded Chicken Pattie, Italian Breaded Chicken Filet, Breaded Chicken Filet, and Chick-on-a-Stick. I never had much success selling my bread filling chicken breasts in the South. I did not figure out why until after I moved to Georgia later in life. The "stuffing" in the South is made with "cornbread" instead of white bread.

When I realized I needed a refrigerated truck, I did not have the money to buy one. My maintenance man and I measured the inside of my truck bed, and we went to the local lumber yard. I bought 4' x 8' x 2' styrofoam panels and secured them to all of the inside surfaces of the truck bed. When a delivery trip was scheduled, the driver would drive to Hurr's Dairy in Williamsport, a nearby town, and pick up dry ice to keep the chicken products cold during delivery. I used this truck for several years to make our deliveries. As the business continued to grow and the loads became bigger, it was clear that I needed a refrigerated unit to keep the products cold.

I began looking for a used refrigerated truck. I had a customer in Uniontown, Pennsylvania, who was selling an old truck with a good refrigeration unit on it. Jerry Blanchard and another employee drove to Uniontown and brought the truck home. Jerry said that it did not go over 40 miles per hour the whole way home, which was about a four hour drive. The refrigeration unit was in good condition, and Jerry transferred the refrigeration unit to the truck that we had been using with the foam insulation.

Jerry parked the old truck out by the roadside near the island bridge, and a farmer came by one day and bought it for $200.

This refrigerated truck was used until it was destroyed in the low overpass accident described earlier in my story. From that time forward, I leased a refrigerated truck until I sold my business.

My plant worked full time because I finally was able to build enough freezer space to hold at least 20 tons of product. I also had refrigerated storage to hold 20 tons of raw product. There were times when it took every last box of product just to fill the orders going out.

We tried to keep enough stock on hand so that none of the customers would be disappointed with their orders. Sometimes, it was difficult to keep going because the cash flow would dry up. The poultry coming in had to be paid for in seven days, if I wanted to be sure that my supply would not be cut off. That meant that I was stockpiling and not having any income because the customer had 10 days with a discount or 30 days before becoming delinquent to pay for the products they bought. Lots of the customers went to the 30 day plan and that is what created the cash flow problem.

Facts about our work

Each breast is selected from U.S. Govt. Inspected Broilers. Boned by our experienced staff and sized to meet your requirements. Nothing but the finest fresh poultry is ever used in our processing. We are covered by USDA. ....

Each item has been carefully studied and tested in our kitchen. Our kitchen is particularly proud of all these items and their eating qualities.

Only prime fresh chicken meat is used, to give you the delicate flavor of poultry.

For a taste tempting treat we invite you to try any one or all of these items . . . .
DELIGHTFUL . . . . Serve them at your next Banquet.

Menu Ideas

Mrs. Warren's Chicken Patties

These tender juicy steaks are made of all white meat, with no fillers added. The meat is chopped, formed, then lightly battered and breaded.

The 3 oz. round is an excellent sandwich item or it can be used as your main entree. The 4 oz. oval makes a delightful luncheon item. The 2½ oz. round, which has a small % of dark meat added can also be used for sandwiches or as a luncheon item.

Cooking Instructions

Do Not Thaw — Do Not Overcook
Deep fat fry at 375°F for 1½ to 2 min. Pan fry 2½ min. on each side at med. heat. Oven bake — Brush with butter, oleo, or cooking oil. Place on cookie sheet in oven pre-heated to 400°F for approximately 20 min. Turn once.

Mrs. Warren's Kiev

Ingredients, skinless white meat of chicken, seasoned, filled with butter, lightly battered and breaded.

Mrs. Warren's Hawaiian

Ingredients, skinless white meat of chicken seasoned and filled with ham and pineapple lightly battered and breaded.

Mrs. Warren's Cordon Bleu

Ingredients, skinless white meat of chicken seasoned and filled with ham and cheese, lightly battered and breaded.

These items are individually wrapped and packed 18 to a carton. Sizes 6 and 7 oz.

Cooking Instructions

Prepare from the freezer. Brown in fat at 375°F. Approx. 3 min. Place in oven for 20 min. at 350-400°F. Can be done in radar range. First brown in deep fat then place in radar range for approx. 12 min.

Mrs. Warren's Filled Chicken Breast

Prepared from portions of all white meat of chicken with skin to hold flavor. Filled with a bread filling, seasoned with herbs and spices. Also done with the herb dressing and wild rice and rices added. These items are prepared in three sizes. 6 oz., 8 oz. and 10 oz.

Mrs. Warren's A-la-Continental

Prepared from portions of all white meat of chicken with skin for flavor and appearance. Filled with a mixture of herbs, seasonings, wild rice and rices. A delightful treat for all.

Cooking Instructions

Pre-heat oven to 350°F. Place frozen filled chicken breast, as they come from the carton, in a shallow baking dish, add a little water. and they will be self basting. Bake for 50 min. Remove foil, brush with butter or oleo and brown for 10 min. Can be browned under the broiler for 2-3 min.

Under Mrs. Warren's Label

We also pack a plain boneless chicken breast. Individually trayed and in sizes 6-7-8-9-10 oz.
On special orders we are packing a 5 or 6 oz. filet of boneless chicken breast, which is a half breast portioned and packed 30 portions to a layer, one or three layer to a carton.

FOR MORE INFORMATION:

PLEASE CONTACT:

ISLAND POULTRY FARM, INC.
P.O. BOX 192
MILL HALL, PENNA. 17751

PHONE (717) 726-4747

THE HOME OF MRS. WARREN'S FROZEN POULTRY PRODUCTS

CHAPTER 41

40 Acres

IN ABOUT 1963, a young man came and offered my father $2,500 for the 40 acres. That was after my father had come to live with me. He said, "Girlie, what do you think I should do?" For some reason, he didn't seem to think that I knew very much. But, he was always consulting me when he had a big decision to make. I told him that I hated to see him sell it. I thought that it would be worth a lot more than that at a later date. He said, "Would you like to have it?" And, I said, "Well, yes I would, but I cannot pay you for it right now," and, he said, "Well girlie, I'm going to give you that 40 acres because I don't think it's worth very much. Since I'm living with you, I will deed it over to you."

The taxes were only $7.50 in 1963, but in 1985 the taxes started going up, and I just didn't know quite what to do. One day, I had a call from a young man offering me $20,000 for the 40 acres. Since I was retired and had no intentions of doing anything with the land, I sold it for the $20,000. The young man did not tell me that he was going to make it into a housing development. But in 2011, while we were visiting in Pennsylvania, I had an opportunity to visit the orchard again, and it was a beautiful development with paved streets, and it was a suburb of Woolrich, Pennsylvania. I could not believe that it was the same piece of property.

CHAPTER 42

Business & Fun Travels

IN 1967, I was at a Restaurant Association meeting, and I heard that they were having their annual meeting in Puerto Rico in February 1968 for a week. Since my daughter, Pat, was graduating from college that spring and was getting married, I thought it would be a good time to go on a trip. I was also told that the trip could be written off on my taxes, since it was business related. I am not sure how much a tax write off would have done for me, since my business was still in the floundering stages at that time, but I needed a break and this was another incentive for me to go on the trip.

I had a good manager, and my only responsibility now was my father. My sister would take care of him for short periods of time, if I took him the 80 miles to her house. Therefore, I made arrangements to go with the group. It was a new experience, since the only traveling I had ever done was for business in the States.

Since I was new to the Restaurant Association, I spent much of that time on my own because I was not very close to any of the folks in the Association at that time. We took a tour from San Juan to St. Thomas where we were stranded for about six hours because of a bad storm in the U.S. that held up the planes coming into the islands. We got back to Puerto Rico and boarded the plane for the U.S. The temperature was 95° when we left Puerto Rico and, when we landed in Philadelphia, it was nine degrees. What a shock!

I had a wonderful time and made new friends and developed a wanderlust for travel that is still with me to this day.

In the fall of 1968, right after Pat was married, I slipped on grain that had been spilled on the walkway as I was leaving the grist mill carrying a 25 pound bag of flour. I crushed my knee in a bad fall. I was able to take care of business from the house but would go into the office when I could finally get around on crutches. Toward the end of my time recuperating, I took my dad and went to California for a week to visit with my daughter and her husband. That was in 1968 before they moved overseas. That was my dad's first ride in a big plane. He was a little reluctant when we first started talking about the trip, but he went anyway and really had a great time and never hesitated getting on a plane again. I kept traveling for the business, doing food shows and working with brokers all over the East Coast.

It was in February of 1972, and I was a member of the Restaurant Association, which was having their convention in Hawaii. I decided that I would go, but I thought that since I was that far, I should try and get a ticket that would allow me to go on to Taiwan and spend some time with my daughter. Her husband was in the military, and they had been living in the Far East for several years.

There were two girl waitresses from Harrisburg, Pennsylvania that came on the trip. I guess maybe that was their first trip away from home because they were not prepared financially for the trip. They did not even have a room and, since I had a real big room with two queen size beds, I told them that they could stay with me. But, it turned out that they did not even have enough money to do the things that we did in Hawaii. So, I ended up sharing my limited amount of money with them. I didn't mind this because it gave me great pleasure to see how much these girls enjoyed themselves. Being waitresses in a small diner in Harrisburg, I did not think they had much money. After touring the islands, I came back from Hilo on the plane and boarded another plane for Taiwan.

Sometime before I left for Hawaii, I had a letter from my daughter telling me that she had a big surprise for me when I got there. You know mothers; I figured right away that I was going to be a grandmother again. The next letter said, "No, Mom, I am not pregnant. That is not the surprise. It is a birthday present." Now, I am excited but did not know why. I never have figured out if I arrived on my birthday, the day before, or the day after with all of the time changes. When I arrived in Taipei and came off the plane, my daughter, Pat, was there with her long flowing blonde hair, amongst all the Asian people, who of course had black hair. When she saw me coming, she started jumping up and down with her hair flying and hollered "Mother, Mother." There were many Asian people there, and they all started chanting and clapping their hands. It was like the Queen Mother had just arrived. I will never forget that glorious feeling of welcome just because I came to see my daughter. They seemed so happy for her. She took me to a hotel and said that I should rest for a while so that she could do a little shopping in Taipei. She wanted to get some things that were not available in the small town where she lived. She said, "Mother, I can't keep this secret any longer." The surprise was a trip to Hong Kong for my birthday. Since I had a trip ticket that allowed me to go from place to place with not much more expense, the cost to go to Hong Kong was only $17 extra. Anyway, after landing in Taipei and resting for a while, we took a long train ride down along the eastern coast of Taiwan, where we reached our destination of Taichung. That night, they had a small birthday celebration for me. That was a wonderful trip, and I have lived it over and over in my mind many times since then. We had a wonderful time in Hong Kong. My daughter decided to have a pair of shoes made while she was there. Since most of the Asian people had small feet and she had bigger ones, it was impossible to buy shoes at the stores, so she had a shoemaker make a pair for her. We ordered a pair of shoes one day and, the next day, they were ready. She tried them on and said to the shoemaker, "They don't fit," and he replied, "Yes, they do." When she insisted that they did not fit, he replied, "Yes, they do, me guarantee." Since the cost of the shoes was so small in U.S. money, she decided to take the shoes.

I visited Taiwan for ten days and had many great experiences. I had to travel from the small town of Taichung to the capital city of Taipei, which was about three hours away by train. I was in the air 22 hours from the time I left Taipei until I landed in Pittsburgh, Pennsylvania. I had a very good friend, who picked me up at the airport and took me home. While I was gone, I had a neighbor take care of my dog. She was glad to take care of him, but he got to running around with a new girlfriend dog that he had found. When I got home, I went over to get the dog and brought him home, thinking that he would be excited to see me. Instead, he went to the door and wanted out. I thought that he was just going to relieve himself. I expected to hear him back at the door in a few minutes. After about half an hour, I began to worry and went looking for him. There was about nine inches of snow on the ground. I was sure that he could not be far. In all of that snow, he had gone to a small village not too far away to see his girlfriend. I got in the car and drove over to the village where the other dog lived and, when my dog heard the car coming down the street, he recognized the noise of the motor and came running after me. From then on, I knew that I had to keep a close eye on that dog.

Another time, I went to Seattle to visit a dear friend that was sent out there for six months to work on a project for Penn State University. We had a great time and ate crab legs until I was afraid I might soon resemble a crab leg.

CHAPTER 43

Hurricane "Agnes" 1972

THE HAWAII/TAIWAN TRIP was in February of 1972, and it was in June of 1972 when we had the big floods that nearly put me under. The business limped along until June 1972.

The good Lord still had his guiding hand on my shoulder, and he must have thought, "This woman is in over her head and needs help." Well, He sent the big flood of June 1972 and really made a disaster of my offices, processing plant and my house.

My dad, who lived with me, was with my sister for the winter in Florida. I felt he might be more comfortable in the warmer climate, since our Pennsylvania winters could be so cold. My girlfriends and I were going to go to Florida to pick up Dad and bring him home. I guess the good Lord must have had other plans for me. It was on the evening before we were to leave for Florida, and the water around the island began to rise rapidly from the effects of Hurricane Agnes.

When I saw that the water was continuing to rise, I sent most of the employees home, and we put up as much product and machinery, etc. as we could to the highest level of the building to save what we could. We were so busy trying to save as much processed product as possible, and get out with our lives, that I forgot to call my friends about the problem and let them know that we would not be going to Florida as planned.

Jerry and Florence were two of my most dependable employees, so they stayed to help me.

My driver in my refrigerated truck was returning from the Pittsburgh delivery run. I did a lot of praying that truck would get home in time for us to get some of our frozen foods loaded on to it to go to a safe frozen storage facility. When he arrived, the water was coming over the banks of the streams in front and in back of the plant and my house. The driver pulled the truck into the loading dock and I told him to jump in his car and leave. Florence and Jerry loaded the truck with all the frozen product that it would hold in order to save it. While they were loading the truck, I went to my house to put up as much furniture as I could carry upstairs. I carried a big console TV up to the landing going to my upstairs area. How I carried it, I don't know to this day. I was just trying to save as much as I could carry.

Finishing all I could do in the house, I waded in knee-deep raging water back down to the plant where Jerry and Florence were working. There was a lot of large debris banging into my legs as I forced my way through the water. When I entered the plant, they both yelled, "The Boss is in the plant." There was about two feet of water in the plant on the lower level at that time. They were glad to see me because they were not sure what to do next. I yelled, "Let's get on the truck and get off this island while we can still get out."

By the time the truck was loaded, the water had washed the gravel from under the wheels of the truck and left the truck hanging on the dock. When Jerry got in it to drive it away, and discovered that all he had was spinning wheels, he jumped out into the rising water, jumped up on the dock, grabbed a big crow bar, and jammed it between the dock and the bumper and gave it a jerk. The truck flew off the dock. Jerry then jumped back in the water, climbed into the cab and started to pull the truck away.

Jerry, Florence, and two of her children were in the cab of the truck, and I was standing on the running board, hanging by the window, with the water lapping around my calves. As we passed my house on the way off the island, I asked Jerry to stop, and we ran into my house and he helped me turn the dining room breakfront upside down on the table to get it up higher. I grabbed my dog, Coco, and we ran back to the truck and headed for the bridge. After we crossed the bridge and started up the road, the water was splashing up over the engine of the truck. All of a sudden, the truck stopped. Jerry said, "Come on Mariah, you can't do this now." He turned the key, and the truck started, even though the water was splashing over the hood of the truck, it continued to pull us up to dry ground.

It was a narrow escape. We finally ended up at Florence's mountain home. She kept the refrigerated truck going until morning when Jerry could get back to take the load to a safe freezer in Altoona. Meantime, my friends didn't know that the trip had been canceled until they got up in the morning and could see the high water from their house. Florence knew a way to get off the mountain to my daughter's home. I walked out and stayed with my daughter until the water went down and we were able to get back to the island and see the destruction that had taken place. My legs were black and blue from the debris that was trying to knock me over when I made the last trip to the plant before we left the island.

When I was able to get to a phone, I called my father and told him that I was wiped out by the flood. He said, "No, you are not, Girlie. You can handle this." He did not know what I was facing. It was several days before I could get back on the island, and what I saw was devastating and overwhelming. I did not know where to start or if I could start.

My son-in-law came up and saw what my needs were and put out a call on the radio asking if someone with batteries could bring them to me. It was only a short while after that when I saw a young man, James P. Webb, Jr. or "Bud" as we all called him, walking across the bridge with the needed batteries. When he saw the condition that the island was in, he said that he would bring up the equipment to fix the large hole in the road (about the size of a car and about three feet deep), and he took a couple of truckloads of debris from around my trees and shrubs. He then came back and took all of the chicken products, approximately ten tons, that could not be saved and took them to a landfill.

A fellow business owner, who owned a local lumber company, brought a large pump with a fire hose attached to the end of it. The water had receded from the plant, leaving about four inches of thick mud. The meadow beside the plant still had water in it from the flood, so we put the pump in the meadow water, and one of my employees and I manned the high pressure hose and hosed out the plant floor and hosed down all of the equipment. Some small items of equipment floated away, but they were not critical to getting started again.

The company, who installed all of my freezers and maintained them over the years, came in and took off every motor, down to the smallest ones, and tagged them and took them to Pittsburgh and distributed them to companies who could dry them and clean them out, so they would work again. When they were workable again, they brought them back and replaced them all. I could not have started my business back without these motors in my automated plant.

After long days at the plant to get it cleaned up for business operation again, I would wearily go to the house with another employee, and she and I would work on getting the two inches of mud out of my house. I was fortunate that the sump pump in my cellar continued to work until the electricity went out and came back on when electricity was restored to continue pumping most of the water out of the cellar. There was two inches of silt on top of my rugs, and we just kept hosing it down with a garden hose until it filtered down through the carpet, hardwood, sub-floor, and rafters. The good old sump pump kept the water flowing out of the cellar as we kept hosing down the carpets to get rid of the silt in the first floor of my house.

If it had not been for Bud, Jerry, my other employees, companies I had done business with for years, and the community at large, I do not know how I would have gotten back on my feet so quickly, if ever!

In the end, there was eight feet of water in the plant, seven feet in my offices and two feet in my house. I never realized that my house was on six feet higher ground than my plant until after the flood. My loss was $120,000. The area was declared a disaster area, and people who were affected by the flood water got $5,000 per household. Since I had previously borrowed money from the small business administration, they loaned me another $72,000 at 1% for my business to start up again.

Since the truck had just returned that day from the Pittsburgh deliveries, our next big runs were not due for two weeks to Philly and the New England states. Fortunately, we had saved enough product to fill all of those orders. That just left us with the task of cleaning up the plant and getting started back up again.

While all of this was going on, the money kept coming in, but the outflow of money stopped. All I had to pay were the people who were helping to get the operation going again. The people that supplied us with product were very uncooperative. Unfortunately, they had just delivered five tons of chicken at 5:00 a.m. the morning of the flood. Their plant manager called me, when the flood water was up around my calves, to tell me that they wanted their money and did not intend to share any of my losses. I said, "Don't worry. You will get all of your money, even if I have to scrub floors to do it." This was the last phone call I got before fleeing the island. We lost all of that product that had to be buried in a landfill.

Fortunately for me, the money started coming in from receivables for all of the previously sold product, so I had more money than I could ever imagine, and none of my creditors lost any money due to me or my business.

We were down for three weeks with just three employees, and all of the receivables were coming in. There was no product going out and little payroll with three employees, so I became well-healed, and we were back in business in three weeks.

Now, all the customers that did not want to buy all their product from me (other companies copied my products), finally decided that if I came through all of that flood difficulty and never missed a delivery, they could count on me being there for the long haul.

Customers who literally bought only 25 boxes of product at a time, began buying 100 boxes at a time. Before the flood, they kept saying

I was a woman and probably would get married and they couldn't afford to put their eggs all in one basket for fear that I would not stay in business after getting married. After the flood, my customers realized that I was a "real player" and that I was in it for the long haul. They all knew that I had the best products around and that their customers always wanted Mrs. Warren's brand. From then on, my business was secure. I came back from that and was more determined than ever to make a success of the business that I had started in 1946.

About six weeks after the flood, when the ground had dried out, a man from the township supervisor's office came to my door and asked if he could go up through the field in back of my house with a very large dump truck full of rocks. I asked him why he wanted to do that. He said that they wanted to shore up the banks of the creek on the top of the island where the flood waters had severely eroded away the bank to prevent further erosion. I told him that I thought it was great that the township was willing do that when I had not asked them for any assistance related to the flood.

A few weeks later, I was looking out my kitchen window in the front of my house, and I saw some surveyors out on the road that came across the bridge onto the island. I went out and asked them what they were doing. They said, "Now, Mrs. Warren, don't you give us a hard time or we will not macadam your road." They said this laughingly. I said, "What do you mean, macadam my road?" They said, "We know how much damage was done to your road during the flood, but you never asked us for any help." Until that time, I did not know that my island road, as it came onto the island, was a township road. They told me that it was township from the end of the bridge past my house and down to a telephone pole that was about 100 yards past my house on the way to my office building.

I always thought it was owned by me and the neighbors who lived in the other house on the island. I imagined a line down the middle, dividing our properties, and we each owned half. That was another unexpected, pleasant surprise arising from the flood damage.

CHAPTER **44**

My Rental Properties

ABOUT SIX WEEKS after they paved the road, the owner of the other house on the island decided to sell her property, and I asked her how much she wanted for it. She told me $10,000. The next day, we went to the lawyer and completed the sale. I then turned the house into a rental property.

The first renters were a young couple who had a large dog. I told them that I really did not want to have a big dog in the house. The young wife said, "Oh, he has been to obedience school and finished 'first' in his class." I said, "Oh, that's nice. How many were in the class?" She replied very proudly, "One."

I let them rent, and they were there for about a year. The dog never did any damage to the house, but when they left and we were cleaning up the house for the next renter, we found at least one inch of dog hair on the carpet outside their bedroom door where the dog slept at night.

It was shortly after that, when I converted the second floor of my office building to an apartment for rent. I rented to a nice young man, who was the assistant principal at the high school from which I graduated. He rented from me for a couple of years, until he got married, and they bought a home of their own. I am still friends with this couple, and we still communicate after 40 years.

The original part of that same building, that had been my plant before I expanded to another building, became another space I could rent out. I rented space to a young lady who wanted the space for making and teaching ceramics. It did not rent for very much money, and she rented it until she developed cancer and died several months after renting it. The next renter of this space was a sculptor, and I never did figure out what he was doing. One time, when I was in the building, he had a casket with a sculpted mummy in it. I never did see any other work that he was supposedly making. He stayed for about six months and left.

After this space did not seem to be working as a rental space, I started a small outlet store for my gourmet chicken products to sell to local customers. Through word of mouth, more and more people were coming to buy my chicken products. I maintained my office in this building, so when customers came to the store, a bell would ring and whoever was working the office would go wait on the customers.

Since we had customers for my gourmet chicken breast products, we also added other frozen food items, like Sexton brand pies, frozen hamburger patties, etc.

First processing plant converted to apartments, offices and a small retail store.

Telephone: (717) 726-4747

MRS. WARREN'S
FROZEN POULTRY PRODUCTS

Louise Warren
FOUNDER

ISLAND POULTRY FARM, INC.
P.O. BOX 192 MILL HALL R.D. 1, PENNA. 17751

CHAPTER 45

"Fund Raising" Again

IN 1973, I had a granddaughter, who was 13 years old, and she belonged to the Rainbow Girls, which was a part of the Masons. They needed money raised to take a trip to Yugoslavia. Of course, I became involved in helping to raise the money. That project was more successful in getting together all of the money needed in less time than the band project. The morning we put her on the bus to leave for the trip, it seemed like we were sending off a little girl, and she was a lovely young lady when she came back two weeks later. She has gone on to be a medical doctor and surgeon.

CHAPTER 46

Trim That Apple Tree

IN ABOUT 1973, when my father was 92 years old, he decided that he was going to trim the apple tree that was out in the meadow. I told him I did not want him to do that because it was not safe for him to be on a ladder. He had been crippled in an accident in his mid-fifties and now used crutches or canes to walk. In discussing this with him, I thought I had squashed that idea. Lo and behold, while I was away one day, he went to the plant and had one of my employees carry a ladder up to the tree. He climbed up and trimmed the tree. I don't know what gave him this idea, but when I came home, he said, "Girly, how does the apple tree look?" I said, "What is the matter with the apple tree?" He said, "I had someone carry a ladder up from the plant and put it up in the tree, and I climbed up and trimmed it." It was fortunate that nothing happened to him because of his age and being crippled, trying to climb up a leaning ladder. I guess maybe I got my determination from him because if anyone told me that I could NOT do something that I wanted to do, I was bound to have my own way!! (At 98 years old, I am still that way!! Just ask my wonderful caregivers.) When I thought I could do something and that it was RIGHT, IT ALWAYS turned out OK. I guess this apple didn't fall far from the tree!

CHAPTER 47

"Union"??? No Way!

IN THE SUMMER of 1974, my plant manager brought a petition to my attention that had been circulated and signed by many of my good employees. When I read the petition, I discovered that someone had infiltrated my work force and was trying to unionize them. I was flabbergasted! I immediately began thinking what I should do about this. I called a meeting of all of the employees to meet in my office, on company time, to let them know that I had received their petition. I asked them why they signed the petition. I also said, "Every time I see some growth in the business, I give you all a small raise, across the board. Never once have any of you said to me that there was a mistake in my check or asked why I had given it to you. Now, I get this petition stating that you want a union. I want to know what you think the problem is that makes you think you need a union." There was no response. I said, "Well, come on now and speak up because there must be some reason why you signed the petition." Finally, one of the last girls that I had hired spoke up and said, "We signed the petition because there are no dispensers in the bathrooms for Kotex." I said, "What else?" No one spoke up with another complaint. I said, "If that is the only issue, I can fix that right away." As they sat watching me, I picked up the telephone receiver and called my paper supplier and asked him to deliver me three sanitary dispensers with a box of sanitary napkins. I said, "There, that complaint is taken care of.

Is there anything else?" There was no response. I went to my desk drawer and pulled out a lock and held it up for all of them to see. I said, "See this lock? If starting a union continues to be a problem, when you come to work the next day, the lock will be on the door, and you will be out of work. If I am going to go to the poor house, I am going to do it sitting in my rocker watching that stream go by and not work this hard doing it."

When I had a chance to have a private conversation with one of my good employees, I asked her why she had signed the petition. She told me that the union girl told her that she HAD to sign it. When I found out for sure who the union infiltrator was, the next day, I changed her position on the line to de-boning chicken breasts. That was the hardest and most demanding job in the plant. It only took two days for that girl to leave. I had always paid my employees above minimum wage after their two week probation period to see if they were able to do the work. After the union girl quit, the union was never brought up again.

CHAPTER **48**

Restaurant Association

IN 1975, THE Restaurant Association's annual meeting was held at a hotel in Philadelphia. Trying to kill two birds with one stone, I bought a one-way ticket into Philly and was met at the airport by my food broker. We were going to work on calling on current customers of mine and try to find a few new customers. After the day's work, he took me to the hotel where the meeting was being held. I was to meet the girl from another region, as representatives of our Association.

While getting dressed to go down to the bar for cocktails and dinner, there was a loud pounding on our door. My nephew was standing there pounding on the door and wanting to enter our room. My roommate told him that we were in the process of getting dressed and that he could not come in. He kept saying loudly, "I want to see my Auntie Louise." She told him that she would call security if he did not go away. He finally left, and we finished dressing and went down to the bar to meet the other members before dinner. I went over and sat down by my sister and her husband, who were also members of the Restaurant Association. A few minutes later, the door to the bar opened and in a loud voice, my nephew said, "Oh, there is my Auntie Louise." He drew the attention of people in the bar around us. He came over and sat down beside me and started using foul language and telling me that I was a thief, a crook and an abuser of my father, who I had taken in to live with me when he could no longer live alone. Next to me, there were five men sitting, and one of them got up and said to me, "You look like such a nice lady, and I cannot understand why you would let anyone talk to you that way." He offered to walk me to my room. I was so shook up that when we got to my room, he asked for the key, opened the door, turned, and walked away.

Since I had flown to Philly on a one-way ticket, I was supposed to return home with my sister and her husband. The next morning, when I got up to check out, I told them at the desk who I was waiting for to take me home. They informed me that they had already checked out and left for home. Fortunately for me, there was another restaurant owner from my area where I lived, and they told me that I could go home with them. They said they were going to stop at the Reading Mall on the way home. That was OK with me, so I went home with them. I don't know what brought all of this on and still do not know to this day, nor do I care.

I was invited to go to Hawaii again with the Motel Association and some of the good friends that I had made at my first food show experience. I went with a dear friend I made through the Motel Association, Bertha Harvey. Bertha owned a small motel near Pittsburgh. We went to see luaus and native dances and a Don Ho show. It was all fun.

Fun in Hawaii!

Bertha Harvey and me in 1975.

CHAPTER **49**

New Island Bridge

IT BECAME APPARENT that the big eighteen wheelers were having a lot of trouble turning onto the bridge at a 45 degree angle in order to hit the plank trail with their tires. The drivers were also afraid that the bridge would collapse because it had been built in about 1850 to accommodate a grist mill that was on the property, and it had a weight limit sign of two tons. It was an overhead iron bridge with a wooden floor. When it was built, there were no cars, and it was built to accommodate horses and wagons that would be bringing grain into the grist mill to be made into flour, buckwheat flour and corn meal. Since bread, cakes, pies, corn bread, buckwheat cakes, etc. were all made from scratch during that era, in each home, the grist mill was an important community asset. The mill was powered by a water wheel, and this was why the island was originally chosen for the grist mill site because water was easily available.

As my business became larger and larger, the trucks bringing in merchandise became larger and larger. The drivers were afraid to come across the bridge. I would have to get up many times at three o'clock in the morning and go out and guide the trucks in over the bridge. One of the drivers said to me one day, "I am afraid that this bridge will collapse and my truck will end up in the water." I tried to reassure him that it would not and, if it did, I would take care of it. I don't know how I intended to take care of it, if it happened, but I was always putting my foot in my mouth. At this point, I was trying to reassure them, so I could get the deliveries I needed for my business. I decided then that I would have to see if I could get the county supervisors to get me a new bridge.

The bridge was pretty well rusted and had been moved about a half an inch off the foundation in the 1972 flood. The truck drivers knew that their rigs and loads weighed more than two tons. The county supervisors checked out the half inch displacement of the bridge and made the determination that the bridge safety was not compromised.

Eventually, I had to send a pickup truck to the other end of the bridge on the highway to off-load these big trucks that would no longer cross the bridge. This would take several trips to off-load my raw chicken products and get them in a cooler. This was not only time consuming, but costly.

My son-in-law, who worked for me, was also active in the local Republican Party. I asked him if he would go with me to a county commissioner's meeting. He and I went to the next meeting, and I told them I was there to ask them if they could install a new bridge onto my island in order to keep my business open. I explained the situation about deliveries onto the island being an issue with my suppliers.

They said they would look into it. Several weeks went by, and one night about nine o'clock, there was a knock at the door, and there stood two of the commissioners. They said, "Mrs. Warren, we cannot authorize a new bridge to accommodate one enterprise using taxpayer dollars." I reminded them that I was the largest employer in the township and that we worked every day and my business was growing. I also told them that I would have to close my business if I could not get a new bridge. They kind of backed off at this point and started putting out contracts for the cost of a new bridge. I told them that I was willing to help pay for the bridge.

I did not know where this money was coming from, but again, I put my foot in my mouth and told them that I would get $12,000 toward the new bridge. The only way I knew how to get this money was to cash in a $10,000 insurance policy that I had for a long time.

The township, the county, the federal government, and I pitched in to come up with the money for the new bridge. They expected the bid to come in at about $83,000. But instead, it came in at $123,000. So, they came back again, and said, "We are sorry, but you will not be able to get the bridge because we do not know where to get the extra money." I said, "Well, I can scrape together another $3,000." They didn't expect to hear me say that, so they said, "Well, maybe we can get the other agencies to chip in a little more to make up the difference." The commissioners were able to get the others to chip in the extra money to make up the additional $37,000. It was reported that the total cost of this project was $144,000, but I was never asked to put in any more money when the bridge was completed.

That is what happened and, in September 1976, the bridge was installed. Heavy stressed concrete was hauled in and put across the creek as a foundation to build a new bridge about 20 feet upstream from the old bridge. They left the original bridge standing, but blocked it off to traffic. Now, the big eighteen wheelers could cross the bridge without any fear. Hooray! What a blessing!

The old bridge stood for about another year, when a local Amish man came and asked how much I would take for the old bridge. I told him he could tear it down and take it away. The Amish men in our community saw the potential for making some money by selling the scrap steel from the old bridge. One day, a crew of Amish men came and started tearing down the old steel bridge, and it was gone in about a week. This left me with only the new bridge. From then on, we had no more problems having the big trucks coming and going across the bridge to deliver and take products.

Now, I'm ready to expand the business even further with the new bridge and the help of the 1972 flood. After getting the new bridge, my business really started to flourish. We had expanded our line of products and were able to use every bit of the chicken meat. By now, we are buying about 25 tons of chicken breasts a week. We no longer could depend on one supplier, so that phase of the business had also changed. We went from buying a few hundred pounds of bread for filling to buying a ton at a time and the same way with our breading materials. By now, we had breading machines, fryers and machines to mix the filling. The mixers were like small concrete mixers but made of stainless steel.

The filling crews were able to do 50 dozen filled chicken breasts an hour, and there were times that we had to set up four lines to keep up with the demand. These ladies were all very proud of the work they did and the product that they produced. They all followed my orders to not put anything in the freezers that they would not want to eat themselves because they all bought so much product that they might be eating it. I allowed them all to buy product at cost. I never made any profit from the purchase of products purchased by employees or relatives. I also never had a case of product returned for refunds because of it being inferior, short weighted or for any other reason. I thought that was a pretty good record after starting the manufacturing of these gourmet chicken products 16 years earlier.

After that, I knew that someday I would be worth a lot of money, after starting out with barely a dime. Without the new bridge, the business would not have prospered and grown. I would not have been able to sell the business in 1980 and fulfill my childhood dream of becoming a millionaire. This would not have been possible if my father had not decided to sell me the island, and it also would not have been possible without my friends and business associates, who had faith in me and gave me credit when I needed it, for whatever reason. I was well respected and trusted in the business community.

It was unfortunate that my nephew had taken my dad away a few weeks before the bridge was completed, and he never got to see the new bridge or celebrate in the ribbon cutting ceremony. I know he was looking forward to that day. After that was when the problems with my family started.

Mrs. Clyde Rishell, secretary/treasurer for the Lamar Township supervisors, received a check for $52,500 from Fred K. Walker, regional representative for the Pennsylvania Department of Commerce, for the construction of the Island Poultry Farm Bridge. Total cost of the projects was $144,000. Pictured from left are: Mrs. Warren, Commissioner Carl W. Kephart, Commissioner John F. Boyle, James J. Petrarca, president of Industrial Development Fund of Clinton County, Mrs. Rishell, Commissioner, William M. Brown, Richard Novesel, vice president and general sales manager of Mrs. Warren's Frozen Poultry Products, Fred K. Walker, Raymond Masser, chairman of Lamar Township Supervisors; Arlington Walizer, Lamar Township Supervisor and Buchanan Ewing, director of Clinton County Development office.

Photo taken by The Express

The new island bridge.

Coming off the island, the old bridge (on left) before the Amish tore it down.

CHAPTER 50

Family Problems

DAD WAS NOT difficult to care for as he was quite fond of my cooking and not a fussy eater. That was until the last two weeks he lived with me. He then began standing over the stove every time I cooked because he declared that I was putting poison in his food. I did not want to believe he was failing and had the beginnings of dementia. I did not realize until much later that he was being told by a relative that I was trying to do him in. He would go to Florida to spend the winters with my sister. This was the same relative who was telling my dad all of these lies. She was being goaded on by other relatives. I found out later that these same relatives were calling my dad and telling him all kinds of things, like I was leaving the tenants of his houses destroy everything. When I found this out, I took my plant manager and went to do a thorough inspection and found things much as they should be in his rental homes.

It was not long after this that these same relatives came to call on Dad and told him that they wanted the big house (Homestead). He said when he passed away the Homestead would be their mother's, but she could not have it until he died. An in-law became very nasty and said, "We want it now," and called my dad some very nasty names. I spoke up and said, "You are only an in-law, so what do you have in this anyway?" Her husband said, "She is saying the things that need to be said that I do not have the guts to say." Well, I could see right there that I had trouble on my hands but did not know how much trouble. She turned to her husband and said, "Well come on, we have our work cut out for us." She looked at me and said, "You have been taking Pappy's money from him all these years." I looked at them and said, "I have borrowed my money from the SBA three different times." The in-law yelled back in response, "LIAR, LIAR, LIAR!" I showed them the door and asked them to leave my home.

Sometime after that, a girlfriend came to me and asked me who owned the Island Poultry Farm. I said, "What a question. You know that I own it and have for over 25 years." She said, "You had better stop your dad from telling people that he owns it." I said, "My dad is going on 96 years of age and, if it makes him happy to think that he owns it, so be it." What I didn't know was that he had been telling my siblings and their children the same thing, and they believed him and decided that they would take it away from me.

It was sometime after talking with my friend about what my dad was telling others that these same relatives came up with the idea to claim the property and everything that I had. They systematically tried to turn my entire family against me.

I couldn't imagine that they thought I was so stupid that I would put all of those years of hard work and money into something that was not mine. I bought the island property from my dad when I sold the first house that I built in 1939 that I lived in with my first husband. Up until 1962, I had been using it as rental property. If they had not been so stupid, they could have gone to the court house and verified that the property was in my name and had been for years.

One afternoon, in September 1976, just before the new bridge was to be commissioned, I came in from work, and I found my father with his suitcase all packed. I asked him where he was going, and he said he was going down to his grandson's house because my sister was going to take him to Florida the next day, and they were going to buy an orange grove. I said, "Dad, she is not going to Florida tomorrow." (She had already moved back to Pennsylvania.) He kept insisting that he was going to Florida, and he got verbally abusive. I called my sister and told her what Dad was saying and asked her if she thought it would be a good idea that she come up and help quiet him down. She said, "I will be right there." Within a half an hour, my sister and her son drove into my driveway and said, "Dad, you don't need to take this damn crap off of her. Come and get in the car." As they were leaving, they stated that they would not allow me to continue to try to kill my dad. They had decided to get everything my dad had, since it had been so easy for my other sister to take everything that my mother had years earlier.

Dad was beginning to fail at that time, and it was only a few days after he left until I got a phone call wanting to know if I had ambulance insurance because they had my dad taken to a hospital. It was not a hospital close to me, but 20 miles away, and they wanted my insurance to pay the bill. It was only five or six weeks until they had my dad in his grave. They demanded that I give them $20,000 that Dad had given me in 1974, when he sold the rental home that was to be my inheritance according to the Will he had made some years before. Dad asked me what he should do with the money, and I told him that I had a loan at the bank for $20,000 and, if he wanted to pay off that loan, I would pay him $150.00 interest on his money every month. I made these payments until they took him away. This really infuriated them and, before he was out of the hospital, they wrote a letter and sent copies to all of the relatives telling them how I had mistreated my dad for the last 16 years and had taken all of his money. They made a big mistake in sending a copy to my daughter in Florida. My daughter called me and read the letter to me. She sent a copy of the letter to me also. My youngest daughter, of all people, knew just how much time and effort I put into making my dad's life enjoyable. When he came to live with us, it was her that gave up her room for him, just at a time when a girl's room is her sanctuary. She gladly gave it up and for the rest of her high school days had to share a room with me. She did it without a complaint and treated my dad with every respect. We never could go any place without taking Dad along and we did. Anyway, after the letter went out, the relative called me one day and said that I was going to do everything that they said, or they were going to call my brother and have him come in, and he was going to tell me what for. I said, "You just call him and tell him to come, if he wants his ass filled with buckshot." You could tell that I was livid. The brother never did come. I think he was chicken.

Several years before this, I had taken my brother in to stay with me when no one else in the family would have anything to do with him. He never even thanked me. He was with me for about four weeks. And, one morning, he took his lunch and never came back. When he found a woman that would take him in to live with her, she didn't know what she was getting into.

When Dad passed away two weeks after Labor Day, I got a phone call from my nephew asking me to pay the funeral expenses. I said, "You are collecting all of the rents, so I guess you will have to take care of the expenses." I had not been consulted about any of the funeral arrangements and was treated as if I was not a part of the family. Even the obituary in the paper did not mention that he had lived with me but that he had made his home with his grandson. Soon after that, I got a phone call from my nephew asking for everything that my dad had. I said that they had the check book and that was it. His next words were, "You will do as we say because we are going to take every Goddamn thing from you that you have." That was an eye opener, and I thought maybe I should go out of town and get myself an attorney. This was a good move because it was not long before I was summoned by their attorney to come to a meeting and sign some papers. They had a paper prepared saying how I had mistreated my dad and had taken all of his money and on and on it went. I had taken my plant manager with me, and we could not believe what we were reading. I declined to sign and said my attorney would have to see those papers. Their attorney was surprised that I was represented by an attorney but agreed to send a copy to my attorney. What he sent was not anything like what we read in his office, so we decided to take it to court. We went through all of the process of having depositions taken and the trial date was set and, the day before the trial, my attorney called and said that they wanted to drop the case. After a lot of headaches and a near nervous breakdown, my lawyers finally convinced them that they were all wrong. That was good news for me because with the pressure of my business and this family mess, it was almost more than I could handle. From that day until this, 41 years later, I have not seen nor bothered with any of the family except the innocent nieces in California. They had no idea what was going on. When my mother and father were gone, and the family treated me the way they had, I felt that I did not owe them one more minute of my thoughts or time. I cannot say that I have not often thought how nice it would be to have a family other than my daughters, grandchildren and great-grandchildren, but they have filled my life with much joy and happiness, so I will be content with what I have.

They took my father's Will and had me cut out entirely. I kept my father for 16 years without a cent of compensation, nor did I expect to be compensated. I figured taking care of my father was only the right thing to do since none of the other family members would help. I would have taken care of my mother too, if my sister hadn't taken her away.

In 1977, my daughter and her husband, who worked for me, were going to a food show in Youngstown, Ohio to represent my products. I was not going along, so I decided that I would pack up and go to see my good friend that I had made from the Motel Association, who lived in the outskirts of Pittsburgh and had a motel there. While I was there I called my brother, who at the time, was living in Ohio. I don't remember the exact conversation, but before we were finished talking, he began to rant and go on at me about the fact that I had given his youngest daughter my daughter's coat, which was like new but too small for her. When his wife died, I had given his little girl the coat because she did not have a coat that fit her. His wife and I traded our children's clothes when they were too small and still like new. His wife was like a sister to me. In fact, she was better to me than my sisters. We always exchanged clothes because they had one girl older than mine and one daughter younger, so it worked out fine for both of us. I suspect that one of my sisters told him about the coat because I don't think he knew about the coat or where it came from or if he even noticed his daughter had a new coat. Anyway, I took these two children down to the children's shop and bought them both new outfits for their mother's funeral. It was even a problem for me to keep my own children dressed in a style that I felt left them well-dressed but was willing to make a sacrifice for these children. I felt so sorry for them. They were 9 and 11 years old and losing their mother. My brother went on with his life just as obnoxious as he was before. I often wondered how we both came from the same parents. I always said, "I don't think I belong to the same family." I think they found me under a stone because I certainly was not like any of the rest of the children. Maybe it was because I was the oldest, and I took the responsibility and did the best that I could to give the children the best of all I had to give.

My father, Clarence Filmore Kryder, Sr., in 1962 at age 82.

My father living with me in 1976.

CHAPTER 51

Chick-on-a-Stick

IN 1976, I developed the chicken-on-a-stick product for an outfit, Charlie Chan, that was starting an oriental franchise chain that was to be sold or be established in malls around the country the next year. This outfit was out of Youngstown, Ohio. A man who was developing the Charlie Chan chains heard that I was in the chicken business and that I was developing unique chicken products. He wanted to know if I could make a chicken on a bamboo skewer for these fast food chains. I started experimenting with this idea and, after several attempts, I finally was able to get just the right amount of garlic in the batter. I used the small pieces of the chicken breast that we removed for portion control on my other chicken products. This was just another way for me to successfully use high quality by-products from my other chicken lines. I set up an assembly line and had my employees putting the chicken pieces on a bamboo skewer and then the filled skewer went down the line and was hand dipped in the batter that I had created using a commercially made batter mix with my own proprietary seasonings. The hard part was getting the garlic additive correct and, by that time, I had figured out exactly what the mixture proportions should be. I bought three commercial deep-fat fryers and had special racks made to hold six skewers, each from the top, so the skewers hung down into the fryer. I figured out how long each rack of six skewers needed to stay in the hot oil and set the timers on the fryers for these automatic times. The racks automatically came up out of the oil when the frying time was up. Each fryer held six skewers, and I had three fryers, so I could make 18 skewers at a time. The fried skewers were laid on a rack to cool and, when cooled enough, they were packed in boxes of 24 skewers. At the height of this franchise, I was shipping 2,000 skewers a week to the distribution center in Youngstown, Ohio where it would be re-distributed to the individual franchises around the country.

Charlie Chan was holding a convention in Youngstown, Ohio in 1977 to attract people to buy their franchises. My son-in-law worked for me at the time, and he and my older daughter went to the convention.

Around 1978, my older daughter said, "What do you think about us buying a Charlie Chan franchise?" I said, "Well, I hope it's a good thing, but I think you're going to be tied down a lot." She said, "Oh no, we are not going to be tied down. We're going to have somebody else run the store, and we're going to make a lot of money." Well, they put it in the hands of 17 and 18 year old kids that knew nothing about running a restaurant or how a business should be run. They had signed a 10-year lease at $1,995 a month. At first, it went very well because they were the only food store in the mall. But, after a few months, other food stores came in and, of course, their sales dropped. I didn't know they were getting farther and farther behind with taxes, rent and any other bills that may have needed to be paid. Finally, they said to me, "We need money because we are getting so far behind with bill paying and taxes to be paid." I told them I would bail them out but that I would not give them money unless I could go down and run it. They agreed, and I was there for about a year and that was when I developed high blood pressure from the stress. And, I have had high blood pressure ever since. I did not set my hours so the employees would not know when I was going to show up. Well, I found out that the business was not being taken care of. One morning, I came in about 10 o'clock, and the restaurant was not open. I opened the store and, after a while, the manager they had hired to run the store came in slinging his briefcase, like a big shot, and asked me what I was doing there. I told him that I came in and opened the restaurant and was taking care of the customers. He started cursing at me and said that he did not have to take this BS off of me, and off he went. He later said that he left because he was not getting manager's pay. Not only was he not managing the store, you could not even say that he worked there. Before I was through getting this place closed, and the taxes and bills paid, it personally cost me $35,000. When my daughter died in 1990, I considered this debt paid in full.

The Charlie Chan franchises lasted about twelve years, and I supplied them with "chick-on-a-stick" during that time. Toward the end of this franchise duration, the man in charge said that he was not able to sell any more franchises unless they had the recipes for my chick-on-a-stick. He sent one of his honchos to my office to ask me for the recipe. This man was dressed in a black silk suit, diamond rings, slick hair, and expensive shoes. I knew right away that they were looking to have someone else manufacture this product for them, probably at a lower cost. I stalled him by saying that I would have to talk with my lawyer about giving away my proprietary recipe. It was a Wednesday afternoon, and the lawyer's office closed at noon, so I told him that I would not be able to get hold of the lawyer that day. He said, "OK, I will go to the hotel and be back to see you in the morning." At 8:00 a.m. the next morning, he came to my office and paced back and forth and asked if I would hurry and call my lawyer. The lawyer's office did not open until 9:00 a.m., at which time, I went to my private office and pretended that I had called the lawyer. I stayed in my office for a short while and then came back and told him that the lawyer said that this recipe was to be sold, not given away. He did not offer to buy the recipe. He said, "Well, what am I going to tell my boss?" I said, "Just tell him that the recipe was not something that I would just give away."

He went off in a huff. I didn't hear any more from them, and they kept buying my products. In 1980, when I sold my business, we were still making the product for them, but I don't know what the new owners of my business may have negotiated with them. Several years after I sold my business, the Charlie Chan franchises went out of business. Many companies tried unsuccessfully to duplicate this unique chicken product.

In 1977, after I became quite prosperous, I decided to keep my money in two separate banks because I did not think it was smart to keep everything in one bank. I was in the bank making a transaction and saw a poster that said they had a CD for interest at 10%. I asked about it and the banker said, "You do not have enough money for one of those." I said, "How much does it take to buy one?" He was kind of rude when he said "$10,000." I just said, "Bye now" and left. About half an hour later, I came back with the money. He was all flustered but fixed the CD and then said real patronizing like, "Can I do anything else for you?" and I said, "Now that you mentioned it, there is something I was thinking. It would be a good idea for me to have a line of credit of $50,000 on hand in case I ever need it." Why sure, he could fix that up for me. Every time I went to the bank after that, he reminded me that I could use the $50,000. I was so far along financially in my business by then that I never had any use for the money.

In 1978, when the business was doing very well, I decided that I wanted to buy a new car and have it customized exactly the way I wanted it. I ordered the color I wanted and all of the features that I wanted. In my whole life, this was the first car that I could pay cash for. After the car was delivered, I drove it down to show it to my good friend. She had visitors, who supposedly were also friends of mine. We all played cards together and often had meals together. My friend and I went out to look at the car and, when we went back into the house, our mutual friend looked out the window, saw the car and turned on his heels and said, "Well, the bank isn't fussy who they go into partnership with." I was so dumb struck that I never replied to his hurting comment. I knew I had paid cash for the car, but it did hurt my feelings, especially coming from him.

The growth of the business became known and that I was deciding to sell and retire. I was fast coming up on 65 years of age and was getting weary of all of the stress. After my family life had been altered in the year of 1976, I decided after not being invited to several family affairs that something radical was wrong, but I did not know what it was. I decided that I would never spend another holiday alone and so went to Florida to spend the Christmas holidays with my youngest daughter from then on.

After doing this a few years, I decided that I liked it in Florida and would buy myself a townhouse. My daughter, who lived in this area of Florida, insisted that I did not need to buy a townhome. Being the independent person that I have always been, I knew that I wanted to spend more time there than I thought appropriate to spend as a guest with my daughter and her husband. I was already thinking how nice it would be to spend six months in Florida and six months in Pennsylvania. Since my 65th birthday was coming up, and I was going to retire, all sorts of visions were in my head for the future.

In the winter of 1979, I went down to the sunny state of Florida for the holidays, intending to stay for six weeks. Since I had a good plant manager, I intended to run my business from Florida. All went well for about four weeks until my plant manager's husband became very ill, and she had to stop working to take care of him. I had to pack up and go home. I really did not want to go home that soon, partly because the business was growing and becoming more stressful, and partly because I wanted to be in Florida where it was warm and not in Pennsylvania where there was ice and snow in the winter months. I felt that I needed the break from the day-to-day operation for a while.

CHAPTER **52**

Selling My Business

ONE DAY IN July of 1980, I had gone to the house for a break, and I got a phone call from the lady who was in charge of the breading operation for my processing plant. We were making chicken patties that day, which required the use of breading material. The day before, we had received a shipment of the breading and, being very busy, we did not have the necessary manpower to spare anyone to go to the storage area and rotate the product as usual. Rotating meant taking out the older material and replacing it with the newest, and then the older material would be in front so that it would be used first. Since we were so rushed, I put pallets down in the hallway and stacked the new breading there. Now, back to the phone call. The woman in charge of this operation said, "Come down here right away because we have weevils in the breading." The first thing I did was inquire who had brought the breading down and where did he get it. He said from the new shipment. This would cause quite a delay in the production because the machine had to be emptied and cleaned before we could proceed. Fortunately, we did have enough old breading stock to get us through that day. I kept the two men that we now had working in our all women's operation after hours and had them remove all of the new shipment out of the building to an overhang in the back of the plant where all of the compressors for the freezers were located. We covered it up with tarps and plastic so there could be no rain damage.

In the meantime, I had called the breading company and put in my complaint. They said that they would have a sanitary engineer in my plant the next day. By the time this gentleman arrived the next day, I was not in a very good mood and, when he came in and started telling me how things were, I said disgustedly, "You know, I am so sick of all of this that I think I might just sell this place."

The "good" sanitary inspector said he could see where the weevils had paths all over my plant, but when I pointed out that the only place we could find it was in the new shipment and went out and opened up a number of the bags to show him, he had to back down and promised me that a new shipment would be there the next day and that the other order would be picked up and returned.

He related my disgusted remark about selling my business to his company and someone there must have thought, "There is a poor little old country bumpkin that I can take advantage of" because it was only a few weeks after the sanitary engineer was there when I got a strange phone call one evening from a man that said he was calling from Lake Wales, Florida.

This phone call was kind of a surprise, since I did not know anyone in that city. He said, "I hear that you live on a beautiful island." I said, "Yes, I think so." He then said, "And, I hear that you have a very good business also." I said, "Yes, I take care of it and it takes care of me." This was kind of casual talk because I had no idea where this conversation was going. Then he said, "I hear that you might be interested in selling." I said, "Yes, if the price is right." Since I had been young and first married, I had a goal to retire at 55 years of age with $1,000,000. Well, here I am 10 years past that goal. When he asked me how much I wanted, the first thing that came out of my mouth was a "$1,000,000." Then he said, "How much do you want down?" I am thinking to myself, one fourth should be enough to keep them from backing out if they were serious. So, $250,000 was the figure I told him for a down payment. Then he said, "I think I have it sold." I am thinking skeptically, yes, that is the way it is done. You just buy something over the phone for a $1,000,000 that you have never seen. So, I forgot about that crazy phone call.

The breading company that I bought from knew that I was doing well because, when I started dealing with them, I was ordering a few hundred pounds of breading material and, in 1980, I was buying it by the tons. After that, things went along smoothly, and my sales continued to grow, and I could see where it was going to be possible to go over the $3,000,000 mark in gross sales by the end of 1980.

About six weeks later, I received another phone call and the man said that he was the person or persons interested in buying my business and could I pick them up at the Lock Haven Airport the following Friday.

I immediately went to a real nice local restaurant and asked them if they would prepare a lunch for me using my products and serve it to us during our meeting. The following Friday arrived, and I picked the gentlemen up and we toured the facility and then I took them to lunch. When we came out of the restaurant, it was a beautiful sunny day, and the Allegheny Mountains that ran the length of the valley were facing us, and it could not have been a more perfect setting for the occasion. As we stopped to admire all of this beauty, I said, "Well, where do we go from here?" I was trying to get some reaction from them because I had not been able to read any reaction from them at this point. The one man said, "We are going to buy." I think I must have been in shock at that point and, of course, not believing what I was hearing. The one man told me that he had his degree in food management and was well qualified to take care of production. The other man was head of a large cafeteria in New York City and had plenty of experience and would become head of the sales force. One man's wife had a big job in some large company, and she would be the business manager. The other wife had a good job as a quality control person in some other plant. It sounded like they had a pretty good thing going and knew what they were doing. A few days later, a lawyer came along and wanted to tour the plant on their behalf. A week or so after that, I had a letter from their lawyer saying that they had changed their offer to $750,000. I called him back and told him that the $1,000,000 was a firm price and there was no room for negotiation, and I would forget the whole thing. Next thing I know, they are back and wanting to draw up a contract. I did not know how much honesty and integrity meant outside of my world until two of the new buyers asked me if I knew what my rating was in Dun & Bradstreet. I told them that I did not belong to that organization. They told me that they had checked and were told that my rating could not be better. What a shock! I knew that I paid off my debts on time and that I did not owe anybody. The federal government had loaned me $72,000 for one percent after the flood of 1972. I had only paid eight years on this debt by the time the new owners wanted to buy the business in 1980. I was able to transfer that debt to them as part of the sale and take it off the sales price of the business. This helped them come up with the $1,000,000 asking price.

My lawyer said not to consider selling right now because in a couple of years it would be worth twice as much. Well, I am thinking, in a couple of years, I might not have a buyer willing to pay cash, and I was getting tired of it all and wanted to retire while I still had my health to enjoy retirement. This was an offer I could not refuse, and I was close to my 65th birthday, so I decided to call it quits. The year before, I had bought a piece of property at Treasure Lake Country Club in Dubois, Pennsylvania, about 75 miles from the island, with the idea that I would someday build a house there for my summer home when I retired. So, I went there and found a contractor and had a little house built and, in three months, I was in my car with my furniture following a U-Haul being pulled by the new owners of my business to my new home in DuBois. I guess they were really anxious to get me off the island.

Over those 35 years that I worked incredibly hard, it never dawned on me that I was doing anything extraordinary other than trying to raise, feed, clothe, and educate my children. They were my primary motivators. Over the years, I remodeled that old shack-like house into a lovely home and kept the island pristine. That day, as I left the island, I looked in the rear view mirror and said "good-bye" to my home and the Island Poultry Farm and have never regretted it for a minute.

The new owners hired me as a consultant for one year as the founder of the Island Poultry Farm to answer any further questions they may have while they were getting used to the business and the daily operation. During that year, I was never consulted once.

About one year later, one of the owners told me that he had heard of the city slicker beating the country bumpkin, but he had never heard of a country bumpkin beating the city slicker. I gave him to understand right then and there that if he would have kept things going the way I had them going when they bought the business, they would have been just fine.

Well, good luck was with me because one of the banks that would not lend me money over the years when I really needed it, took on their loan after seven years. I held the first mortgage at prime plus two percent for seven years with the property and business as collateral. They made up the balance of the down payment in cash by selling various properties they owned in New York. In order for them to get new financing on the business to get more working capital, they had to pay off the first mortgage they owed me. I was advised to consider the tax consequences of taking this settlement, but I believed in the old saying, "A bird in the hand is worth two in the bush," and lucky for me because it was only six years after this refinance that they went bankrupt. The business and island that they paid $1,000,000 for now went at auction for less than $75,000.

My retirement picture when I was age 65.

CHAPTER **53**

Retirement

WHEN I RETIRED, I expected the good life, and it certainly turned out that way. I started my new life in a new home in the mountains at Treasure Lake, Pennsylvania. I did not know anyone in the development, except my sales person and the builder. There was a nice country club and meeting folks there was easy since that was where everyone went when they had a spare evening. We often had our dinners there.

It was there that I met the first man that I had in my life for the past 35 years. Joe happened to be the man that carried the insurance on my property. I had never met him before because it was his son that was my contact during all of the business related to the insurance. Anyway, he started calling on me, and I grew quite fond of him. We always seemed to have a very good time together.

I took up golf and bridge as new endeavors in my life to make sure that I did not get bored. Neither of these games are easy ones to master, but I certainly had a good time trying. We had two 18 hole golf courses on the 100,000 acres of mountain property. It was an impressive project, along with a ski lodge and slopes, stables for riding, a beach, and a very large lake for boats and water skiing. It did not take long for me to find friends to play golf and bridge with. My little house was very well suited to entertaining, and I did lots of that.

If there was not a party going on or a bridge game or a golf game, I would get one started. In business, I was always around many people, so I was not used to being alone. I was bored very easily, and I met a dear friend by the name of Mary Kline. We did lots of things together. We did many things as a group. I had many friends, who would come out and spend weekends with me. These were the friends, who encouraged and gave support to me during my working years. Without them, I would not have made it this far.

In November 1980, I took off for my townhouse that I had bought the year before in Fern Park, Florida. I was also faced with making new friends in Florida. My only connection there was my younger daughter and her husband. They were a busy working family so did not have a lot of time to spend with me, which was as it should be. I did not make the move to Florida with the idea of depending on them for my social life or my everyday living. They were wonderful, and we had a lot of good times together. Disney World was a newly opened attraction then, so I did get a lot of friends visiting from the North and almost all meant a trip to that attraction, as well as Sea World and Cypress Gardens.

I met another wonderful friend and neighbor, Mary McCardle, and she and I decided to take a cruise in the Caribbean. She said it was a very cheap, last minute deal because the ship had not sold out. Not knowing anything about a ship, I did not realize that being on the bottom room floor of the ship was also way under the water line. That was an eye-opener for me, and I decided that I would never take a cruise again "under water." I am thankful that cruise was for only three days, but it was enough to open my eyes to the adventures that would come.

We also took a bus trip to Hollywood, Florida to see a famous Hollywood celebrity, Burt Reynolds, who had opened an actor's playhouse there because that is where he lived.

It was shortly after that I met my dear friend, Norma Schaffner. Not long after I arrived in Florida, my next door neighbors asked me to go to the Presbyterian Church with them. They were wonderful neighbors and invited me to join them on Sunday mornings and also to go to Circle meetings with her.

The Ladies Guild was having a big Christmas dinner that year, and my nextdoor neighbor took me to the dinner as her guest. There were about 30 of us in attendance, and the lady in charge said, "I don't think everybody knows each other, so let's each tell our name and where we are from." The first person to say her name was Ruth Schaffner, and she said she was from Clearfield, Pennsylvania. That town was just 12 miles from where I built my new summer home. As we went around the room and it finally came to me, I said, "I am from Treasure Lake Country Club in DuBois, Pennsylvania, and my name is Louise Warren." Right away, she came running over to me and she said, "You live close to where I live in Pennsylvania." She said, "You know, I've just been thinking. I'm down here with my sister-in-law, Norma Shaffner, and she doesn't have anybody to play golf with or bridge. I know that she's lonesome." She asked me if I played either game, and I told her that I golfed and played bridge. I said, "Well, I have a tee time for tomorrow morning at 10 o'clock, if she would like to go with me. I would love to meet her." I didn't know it, but they came up that night and drove around to find out where I lived. Early the next morning, before 10 o'clock, Norma showed up at my door, and she said, "I'm Norma Schaffner, and I would like to play golf with you." We started playing golf and then we started playing bridge, going out to eat, going to dinner theaters, art shows, and anything that sounded like fun. Of course, Ruth was always included in the things that she enjoyed. Ruth did not play golf or bridge, but we included her in all of the other activities that she would enjoy. We became fast friends and played golf and bridge as many as five days a week. When we first met, it was like we were soulmates. Her friendship was one of the best I have ever had in my life.

In 1983, Norma and I decided to take a trip to Greece. We flew to Athens and boarded a ship to cruise the Mediterranean for 10 days. We then came back into port and toured other parts of Greece by bu.. We rode donkeys, went to see monasteries in the mountains, toured the Greek ruins, went to see the original Olympic flame, and ate lots of wonderful food.

On one of our first meals, we saw other people being served this dish and, it looked like a great dessert, so we each ordered one after our main meal. The laugh was on us when it was served, and we discovered that Moussaka is an authentic Greek entrée filled with mashed potatoes and eggplant. It was very good, but we never ordered it for dessert again. We had eggplant in one form or another at almost every meal while in Greece, even breakfast.

We crossed one of the islands by bus and went up into the mountains where we saw the monasteries on the very tips of high, thin mountains. It was hard to believe that these people would dedicate their life to their religion. These monks were totally isolated and did not speak and had their food delivered by baskets pulled up on pulleys. To get from one monastery peak to another, we were carried by a tram that hung in the air high above the ground. We had a wonderful time. When I came back, I had decided that I had seen enough ruins to last me for the rest of my life. Later you will see that resolve was not to last.

Through my friendship with Norma, I met another dear friend, Tillie Fullington, who was Norma's sister. I was a big Penn State fan and so were Tillie and her husband. From 1967 to 1980, there was a group of us ladies, who tailgated Penn State football games until I retired. I was a season ticket holder for 13 years, at which time I passed my tickets on to my older daughter and her husband. By then, our group had grown to seven ladies, and every game we prepared a good meal. We went very early to the game to find a good spot to have our picnic and socialize until time for the game.

When I met Tillie, she and her husband tailgated at Penn State games, and I was invited to join them. They owned a big bus line, and they had 50 seats on the 50 yard line at Penn State stadium, and they always had a ticket to sell me for the game.

After that, when I went down to visit in Florida, we would go to Sanibel Island for a week with one of my longtime friends, Ada Wolfe, whose mother had rented an apartment there. That was always a good time.

Ada Wolfe and I decided to take a trip to Panama City in the Canal Zone and stayed at a hotel. We took many tours and saw many ruins. Then, we got on a ship and sailed out into the Pacific, disembarked in dug-out canoes and were taken up river a few miles, and then we walked another mile until we came to the Darien Jungle, and we proceeded to go up in the mountains with a guide. That was an eye-opener since all of the people there were only wearing loin clothes, which reminded me of a fig leaf. The reason for them running naked was because the average temperatures were over 100 degrees. When we came back down the river in the dug-out canoes and went to our ship, we climbed up the same rope ladders that we had come down on when we left the ship. When we came back from that, we went through the Panama Canal and came out in the Atlantic Ocean. We visited a small island where the San Blas Indians lived. It was very crude living, according to our standards, and the people were very small. Most of them were not more than 30 inches tall, but they were nice and friendly, and we enjoyed seeing that there was another part of the world beyond what we were used to. We took a small gage train back to Panama City. The next day we flew home.

The Junior Chamber of Commerce was having their convention in Jamaica. My older daughter and her husband wanted to go on this trip, so I helped them financially so they could go. Ada Wolfe said she would like to go, so we signed up for the trip also. A few days later, my friend Joe said he would like to take the trip also, so the five of us went and had a good time. We took a couple of suitcases of medical supplies to the Kiwanis to be used on the island. The President of the Jamaican Kiwanis invited all of us to his house for a dinner. After we had dinner, I asked him what the wonderful meat was that we had for dinner. He said that it was goat, and that was the first time I had ever eaten goat meat. If I had known in advance that the meat was goat, I probably would not have been able to eat it. My friendship with Norma lasted for 14 years, when she developed cancer and only lasted about 11 months.

Shortly before that I had lost my first born daughter to the same disease and was not over the heartache of that loss when this other tragedy hit. I never have quite gotten over either of these loses. My daughter left me with three of the greatest grandchildren, and now they have blessed me with seven of the greatest great-grandchildren. Do I sound like a very proud mother, grandmother and great-grandmother?

Joe visited me in Florida at my condo. He was always worried that I had more money than he had. Someone had told him that I had money. I do not think he knew how much but, out of the blue, he would comment that he bet he was worth a half million dollars. I always said I do not know how much I have. I think he was trying to get me to tell him how large my portfolio was. I had no intention of doing that.

After the Jamaica trip, I stayed at my condo in Florida, and Joe went back to Pennsylvania. For some reason, he was not happy about something when he went back home, and he told one of my friends that he was damn glad to be back home. My friend called me and told me about his comment. I did not know what he meant by that remark. Subsequently, we did not see each other for about a year.

One day, when I was traveling from Mill Hall, Pennsylvania where my business had been located and where my older daughter lived to my home in Treasure Lake, Pennsylvania, I looked in my rear view mirror and saw that Joe was behind me. When I got to my house and pulled into my driveway, Joe followed. I invited him in for a cup of coffee, and we talked like we had never been apart for that year.

He said that he wanted to be friends again and, when he found out that I had a trip planned to sail to Alaska, he decided that was something that he wanted to do also, so on that trip I had my first male companion. We had a good time, but by now his health was beginning to fail, and his illness was really much worse than I had realized. His health condition put a little bit of a damper on some of the traveling that we should have done off the ship. Soon after the trip was when the final break-up came for him and me. By then, he was on oxygen and his health seemed to be failing quickly. I do not know for sure, but rather suspect that he did not want to burden me with his ill health, so he took off for the last time. Later that winter while I was in Florida, I got the phone call telling me that he had passed away. Life went on, but I must say that I missed this man because I had grown quite fond of him.

In July, 1983, I decided that it would be a good thing to get the family together for a nice vacation. I made arrangements for the three couples in Pennsylvania to fly to Florida, so we could take a cruise of the Eastern Caribbean. My younger daughter and I lived in Florida, so we were able to put them all up overnight. The next day, with the help of my cousin, Golda, her husband, Dick, and a kind neighbor, we were all taken to the cruise ship, which was docked at Port Canaveral, Florida. We boarded the ship and then the fun began. After a farewell from the crowd on the docks, we began the cruise. During the days, we stopped at several islands and we could tour, shop, snorkel, or just lay on the beach. In the evenings, we were entertained by the entertainment crew.

My older daughter and her daughter shared the same birthday, so the captain arranged for all of us to be at one table for a celebration. I remember that I got diamond earrings for my daughter, but I do not recollect what I gave to my granddaughter. We all had such a good time and, afterwards, my grandchildren told me that it was the best vacation they ever had. This was the first time any of them had been on a cruise, so it was a special time back then. They bought me a beautiful sweater as a thank you for the trip. This was a wonderful time for me with my family.

We had such a good time on the family cruise that my younger daughter and I decided to go on a week cruise over Christmas and New Years of that same year. Unfortunately, that year, it was one of the coldest winter storms in history that reached all the way south to Florida and beyond.

A few days before the trip, it was forewarned that the weather would be freezing in Florida. We left out of Port Canaveral and thought it would be warm in the tropics where we were going. We decided to take Dramamine before getting on the boat and took along extra pills for the trip. What a trip! We packed light clothes and only had one dress jacket between us. When we planned the trip, we decided that we would not be in our room very much, so we got the cheaper, smaller, inner cabin with no windows. The boat left shore and, when we got about 15 miles from shore, the storm started and continued to be rough and cold the whole time we were on the cruise. On the roughest days, passengers were throwing up all over the staircases and steps. We never got sick because we took our Dramamine that we had taken with us. The ship's staff was handing out Dramamine to anyone who needed it. Most of the shows were canceled because the ship was rolling so much in the high seas that the entertainers could not stand upright on stage. The few shows that were put on were like a comedy show with the audience swaying in their seats as they tried to follow the different acts back and forth across the swaying stage.

At one point, we were cold enough to vie for the one jacket we had between us. Instead, we went to our room and huddled under wool blankets and played gin rummy. At one point, we started laughing over our ridiculous situation and I said, "The next time we decide to spend $5,000 on a cruise, let's just turn on the air conditioning, go into my walk-in closet, huddle in wool blankets, play gin, and pretend we are on a cruise." This was our attempt to keep our sense of humor in a not so fun situation. Most of the ports of call trips were canceled because the seas were so rough that they could not safely get the ship close enough to its tender to get people off and on the ship. On a cruise back then, when there were ports of call, very few, if any, activities were planned on the ship. Obviously, in 1983, these cruises were not the mega-cruisers of later years. The other thing we did not think about when booking this cruise was that it would be made up of families for the holidays. On New Year's Eve, the seas were a little calmer, and they had a dance party. After sitting for an hour with no partner to dance with, my daughter looked at me and said, "Want to dance?" We had a good laugh about this evening. Over the years, we have gone on many cruises and have never had that kind of experience again.

My home after retirement from the island at Treasure Lake, Pennsylvania.

My dear friend, Mary McCardle.

*Fun on the cruise
with Mary McCardle.*

Riding a donkey in Greece.

Me and my daughter, Pat, on the cold Christmas cruise in 1983. My daughter is wearing the only jacket we had with us.

Joe and me in 1984.

CHAPTER **54**

The Cottage Restaurant

OUR LOCAL PHARMACIST owned a piece of property with a restaurant on it and was not able to get rid of it for quite some time. He and my son-in-law were talking one day, and he said if my son-in-law and his wife wanted to start a restaurant, he would let them have his vacant restaurant for a year without paying any rent. My daughter called and wanted to know if I thought it was a good idea. I told her, "You have nothing to lose." And she said, "We don't know where to start and have no money." I told her that I would invest up to $20,000 in the business, but I wanted to be a partner in the business for my investment. My CPA drew up the papers, and I was a partner in the business. They went up and started to clean the building, which had been closed down for about five years. It was a mess and took a lot of cleaning and getting ready to open the doors for business. After about three weeks, my daughter called me again and said, "Mom, would you come down from your vacation home and help us get the place in order?" That was not on my agenda, but I told her that I would come. When I arrived, there were three young men in their teens with a boom box having a really good time and drawing a paycheck for doing nothing. They needed some guidance. When I went in, I said, "I am here to see that this work gets done." They informed me that I was not their boss. I said, "You had better look at the signature on your paycheck the next time you get one." I assigned each one a job, and it wasn't long until we had the building in shape.

On one of my visits, I noticed that there was a curtainless window on the second floor. I had cottage curtains I had used in my old kitchen on the island. I had saved them, so I got them starched and ironed and hung them at that window. When I saw my daughter later that day, I said, "I have an idea for the name of the new restaurant." She asked, "What is it?" I told her "The Cottage Restaurant." So, this is how it got its name and has retained this name until this present day.

People started coming the very next day after opening, but it was not making enough profit to keep Jean's family financially, pay the employees and pay for the supplies. This went on for about a year, and I did not expect any more of it because I knew that it would take a year or so for it to be a profitable business. About that time, my daughter called again and said that the highway department wanted them to put a sign at the exit that came off right at their business from Rte. 80. She asked me what I thought. I told her that she and her husband should do that in order to pull travelers off the exit to their restaurant. The cost was $5,000. She said, "But, we do not have that much money left after everything else is paid." I told her I would give them the $5,000 to have the sign put up. After that, their business progressed well. After about two years, I signed my part of the business over to my daughter and her husband, so they were the sole owners.

When my daughter passed away in 1990, her husband ran the restaurant for about another 10 years. At that time, he was able to find a buyer, sold the restaurant and retired.

The Cottage Restaurant in Lamar, Pennsylvania.

CHAPTER 55

Meeting a Gentle Man

IN 1987, I finally met the man who was my constant companion for the next 19 years.

One Sunday morning, I was at the Cottage Restaurant helping out in the back, when one of the waitresses came back into the kitchen and said that there was a man out front who was asking for me and that he lived in the same Country Club where I was living. I looked out and said, "I don't know that man." She said, "Well, he knows you, so you had better go out." I went out and introduced myself and he did the same. He wanted me to have a cup of coffee with him. The waitress brought me coffee, and we talked while eating the apple dumpling that he had ordered.

He wanted to know if I played golf. I found out much later in the relationship that he already knew that I golfed and that I was not seeing anyone. Over the last two years, he and his wife would stop in the Cottage on their way to visit his ailing mother. While in the restaurant one day, my son-in-law saw his Country Club emblem on his jacket and told him that his mother-in-law lived in that same development. It was some time after that his wife passed away, and the day that he was in the restaurant and asked for me, he was on his way home from burying his mother.

He asked if I would play golf with him sometime. Since I was always on the lookout for an excuse to play, I said, "Yes, I would when

I was in residence." After I was home a few days later, I called him and we set up a tee time and we were off. The next weekend, he called and invited me to play with his son and his son's girlfriend, and we went back to the house later for a cook out. One thing led to another, and it was time for me to go back to Florida for the winter.

He said, "What will I do if you leave?" I really had not given that any thought, but he indicated that he would like to go also. I told him that I was going down for two weeks with a stop in Atlanta to visit my younger daughter and then would be going on to Florida to my condo in Fern Park. I said to him, "If you would like, you can go down with me to see how you like it." The trip went well, and he kept me entertained with stories of his life and family. Later, when I went down for the winter, he went along and we golfed with my friends there and spent at least four days a week on the golf courses, and our evenings were spent dining out and going to see stage productions. He also was learning to play bridge so as not to be left out of anything. I had told him he either learned to play bridge or he would be spending a lot of time at the house alone. When I retired, the two things that I was determined to do was play golf and play bridge and nothing was going to keep me from doing that. Learning to play bridge was not something that he really wanted to do, but the pressure was on, and he gave into it. He became quite a good bridge player, but I was never quite sure if he was crazy about the game.

Bill really enjoyed golf, so he and my friends Norma Schaffner and Gene Williams and I were on the golf course almost every day while in Florida and also back in Pennsylvania, where they both lived in Clearfield, Pennsylvania.

Gene, Norma, Bill, and me.

Norma and me golfing.

CHAPTER **56**

Dick & Tillie

I GOT TO know Norma's sister, Tillie Fulllington, and her husband, Dick. They owned a large bus company and took many tours all over the U.S. and Canada. Dick was very involved in all of the national and state bus associations. While he attended to business, Tillie and I would shop and do some sightseeing that we could do by foot, since Dick and Bill took the car to attend meetings, etc. Dick and Bill would go their way, and we would be on our own for the day. However, we did get to go to the lavish dinner parties every night. Dick was a very good driver and, never once on a two or three thousand mile trip, would he let anyone else drive. Tillie and I would always have plenty of goodies to eat and kept well fueled.

When Bill and I were not on the bus with them, we were in their big GMC traveling across the U.S. We visited many cities and had great times. If there was some place that you even thought about visiting and mentioned it, we were on our way. Dick would say, "Get out the map, find out where we are and where we need to turn off to detour to this new destination." Dick and Tillie took us to such places as Pebble Beach, California; Dallas and Brownsville, Texas; Tucson, Arizona and many more historic places across the U.S. We hit most of the major cities, since each crossing of this great country of ours was done by a different route. They were always so gracious and never hesitated to drive a few hundred miles if there was something that we showed any interest in doing. One trip, we left our original route and drove north to see a dear niece of mine that lived in Bishop, California. Bishop is located far up in the Sierras, and then we crossed over to Tahoe and then down to The Lodge at Pebble Beach. After spending four days at Pebble Beach, we traveled all the way down the coast to San Diego, where we visited my other niece and her family, who is the sister of my niece in Bishop, California.

From there, we took the Southern route home to Florida with many stops. One of these stops was in Biloxi, Mississippi. That trip lasted almost 3 weeks.

It was on one of these trips that Tillie told us about a quaint town that she had read about. Right away Dick said, "Get out the map and see how close we are to this place." Well, it turned out to be about one hundred miles out of our way, and then we had to turn off the highway and go another forty miles. So, off we went and, when we came to what was to be the city limits, did we get a surprise! It consisted of not more than twenty houses, a barber shop and beauty salon all-in-one, a grocery store, and a hardware store. There was another tiny shop with a sign above it saying it was an iron shop. On the trip, I was looking for an iron weather vane for my summer home. Not knowing what to expect, we decided to check it out. Dick pulled up in front of the building and we all got out and went up to the door. This is what we found. It was a sign on the door giving us the opening hours. It read like this:

"OFFICE HOURS"
Open Most Days, about 9 or 10
Occasionally as early as 7, but some days as late as 12 or 1
We close about 5:30 or 6
Occasionally about 3 or 6
But sometimes as late as 11 or 12
Some days or afternoons we are not here at all
Lately, I have been here all the time,
except when I am someplace else,
but I should be here then, too.

That certainly was not the place to make my purchase. However I finally did manage to find the weather vane I was looking for, but I cannot remember where I found it.

Dick and Tillie would also come to Florida to visit, and we would go to many interesting places. Dick always did all of the driving, so his wife, Bill and I, were always the privileged passengers.

I met these lovely folks through two of my dearest friends, who were Tillie's sister, Norma Shaffner, and her sister-in-law, Ruth Shaffner. I loved them both dearly and, since then, they have all passed away.

Bill's sister and husband lived in California and we went out and spent time with them several times. On one of our visits, we went to his sister's time-share at Lawrence Welk Village and my niece, who lives in Fallbrook, California, met us at the village, and I took her and her husband to a show at the village to celebrate our visit.

Dick and Tillie next to the first commercial vehicle they owned when they started their bus line.

My dear nieces, Norma and Diana, who live in California.

CHAPTER 57

Losing My Daughter, Jean

I HAD A house under construction in Florida in 1990 and, when I died, this home was to be for my older daughter, Jean. My Pennsylvania house was to be for my younger daughter, Pat. I thought it would make a nice vacation place for each one of them. My dear daughter, Jean, passed away from metastatic breast cancer in October 1990. Jean's passing ended that dream of leaving each daughter a home. Not many of my plans in life have gone astray, but that one certainly did. I do not know why she was taken from us so early in her life at 55 years of age. I discovered that there is no greater loss in this world than the loss of your child.

She was a good Christian girl and raised a lovely family. She had a boy and two girls, and they have all done very well and have lovely families, of which I'm very proud. My other daughter is close to me here in Georgia, and we see each other often, and the rest of the families are scattered. My grandson and his lovely family live in Delaware. My two granddaughters live in St. Augustine, Florida. We visit each other quite often.

The following poem was written by Ashley Jean Maetozo, reflecting on her grandmother, Jean Louise Novosel, who left this world in 1990, shortly before Ashley was born.

"Her Favorite Shell"

Yesterday while on the beach I found a pretty shell
I couldn't wait to show my Mom, I couldn't wait to tell
About the little object I held in my right hand
It's smooth and shiny and the color of sand
You see this shell is special, it means so much to me
Because it was the favorite of my Grandma Jeani
I never knew her smile; I never knew her love
She left this earth before I came; she took flight like a dove
But I could feel her warmth in the sun that shone that day
I felt her touch in the breeze as I ran on the beach to play
I know she smiled in heaven as I stood upon the sand
And spied the pretty little shell and cupped it in my hand.

CHAPTER 58

Palm Coast Home

WE DECIDED THAT the town house in Central Florida was too small for Bill and me. We went farther north to a growing community called Palm Coast. We found a piece of land that we liked, and I decided to purchase it, and built a house on it. The home was all on one level, with two bedrooms and two bathrooms. When you walked through the front door, you looked through the family room straight out to a large screened-in area with a pool and Jacuzzi hot tub. It was a beautiful house, and we spent ten wonderful years there. We played golf, bridge and entertained a lot.

In the spring of 1998, Bill came home from playing golf and said that he had seen a sign at the golf course asking for volunteers to assist at the new World Golf Hall of Fame in St. Augustine, Florida. We decided that it would be interesting to be in on the ground floor of this new project, so we signed up. We had to go up to the new auditorium at the new World Golf Village. This was 24 miles from Palm Coast were we lived. We went to the orientation, found out what was expected and what kind of uniform we should wear. We were supposed to wear tan slacks, white shirts and tan tie-up shoes. They gave us a scarf to wear with the World Golf Village logo on it and a pin that we wore that designated us as "volunteers." They had their Grand Opening on May 19, 1998. We volunteered every Thursday from 8:00 a.m. to 5:00 p.m. We were assigned different positions each week to interact with the public that was going through the Hall of Fame. My back was starting to really bother me if I stood too long, so they assigned me positions that required mostly sitting duties like "receptionist." We worked in the I-Max theatre, in the game areas and collected tickets and acted as greeters to the public.

When they had the Grand Opening and any other yearly inductions, we were there and met some of the biggest names and legends in golf that were still alive. I remember meeting Gene Sarazen, ChiChi Rodríguez, Arnie Palmer, Jack Nicklaus, Payne Stewart, just to "name drop" a few. We volunteered for two years until our health prevented us from continuing. It is a fond memory, and I am so glad we decided to try this new adventure.

My Palm Coast, Florida home.

Fun in the Jacuzzi at my Palm Coast home.
L to R: Me, Norma, Terry, Gene, and Bill.

CHAPTER 59

More Fun Trips

AFTER TOURING THE U.S. with Dick and Tillie, our next trips were with my younger daughter and her husband. He also had the wanderlust, and we traveled with them many places. The first time, in 1992, we went overseas and landed in Munich, Germany. We rented a car and went on to Austria. We toured there and saw many castles, and then went on to Italy, and then back to France and Switzerland, and back again to Germany, and then back home.

We left again for Scotland with my daughter and her husband, in 1994, for ten days. I never saw so many sheep in all my life, and I certainly wanted to bring a pair of the little ones home with me. Of course, I knew that this was not possible. I would have to remember them as being part of the pleasure of being in Scotland. Again, we saw many ruins, and Pat and her husband played golf while over there. Bill and I did not venture to play golf, and we just walked around the towns to enjoy the atmosphere and the people. That was the last of our trips to Europe.

In 1996, we went to Cape Cod and landed in Boston, got a rental car and drove all the way up the coast to Bar Harbor. We stayed at bed and breakfast inns, and it was over the Fourth of July. The weather was chilly and rainy, and we saw fireworks at Bar Harbor through flashing colored clouds. Then, we went a little further south, and took a boat out onto the Atlantic Ocean near the coast line and watched fireworks over the water. It was cold and the boat ride was bumpy! On this trip, we ate lobster until we couldn't eat any more. It was fun to go to the lobster houses and eat on picnic tables with paper on them and holes in the table through which we discarded our lobster remains.

A few years later, we went to the Canadian Rockies with my daughter and her husband. On the Fourth of July, we were up in the mountains and were in a snowstorm of about four inches. We had to stay in Jasper all night before we could get back down to Banff. We saw a lot of elk and moose on this trip. We stopped at Lake Louise on the way up to Jasper and, of course, I thought they had named this beautiful, azure blue, crystal glacier lake after me! That was our last trip because our backs and legs could not withstand the rigors of that kind of long distance travel anymore.

It was early in the 1990s, when I decided that if Bill and I lived past 2000, we would be happy. But, in 1999, I received a phone call from my daughter telling us that there were several other couples that were going to go to the Greystone Inn in the mountains of North Carolina on Lake Toxaway to celebrate the millennium, and she invited us to go with them. I thought it was nice that these young people wanted to include old folks like us. My daughter said the cost would be $300 per night, I think that was per person because my bill came to $2,100.

Right away, Bill said that it was too much money to spend just to stay at an inn. I said, "Bill, we certainly are not going to live another hundred years, so this will be the last millennium we will see, and we are going to go." Of course, seeing that I had made up my mind the way it was going to be, we got ready and, at the appointed time, we went to Atlanta where my daughter lived. We went, and the rooms were all antique, and the beds were so high that they had to have a couple of steps for us to get into them.

When we arrived at the hotel, we went to our rooms, unpacked and went back downstairs for cocktails and dinner. A woman, who was a guest, started playing the piano, and we all stood around and sang and enjoyed her impromptu recital while we enjoyed our cocktails. We also went on a river ride while we were there (chilly ride) and saw the beautiful homes on the lake. The younger people went to play golf one morning, and Bill and I stayed in the inn, had tea on the veranda and enjoyed the atmosphere.

The night of New Year's Eve, Pat and I were a little late coming downstairs. As we started down the stairs, at the landing half way down the stairs, the whole crowd of people who were milling around, including our folks, just looked up at us and were perfectly still watching us descend the remaining stairs. Later, Pat and I both said that we had an overwhelming feeling that we were somehow "special," like royalty, at that moment. That was the second time in my life that I had felt such an experience. Neither one of us have ever been able to figure out just what that meant, when we both had the same regal feeling for a few seconds. We joined the group and had a wonderful evening and celebration of the millennium. They had a nice band and the young folks danced, and we wore New Year's Eve hats and celebrated when it turned midnight 2000. At midnight, we went outside to watch the beautiful fireworks and see in the new year. The next day, we packed up and went back to Atlanta. What a great way for us to spend that holiday so close to what we thought would be the end of our lives. Bill lived until the year of 2006. I'm still here in 2014 and 98 years old.

Pat, Bill and me in Venice, Italy.

*Bill and me at the millennium party at the Greystone
Inn, Lake Toxaway, North Carolina.*

CHAPTER 60

Vilano Village Condo

IN THE YEAR 2000, Bill and I were living in a beautiful home in Palm Coast, Florida. His health started to fail, and we were not able to keep up the house by ourselves and just felt it was a burden we no longer wanted. I decided to sell and move to a townhouse in Vilano Village in St. Augustine, Florida. This was the same neighborhood where my granddaughter lived, so I wanted to be closer to her if we needed help. Our doctors were all in St. Augustine also, so it made it easier when either of us had a doctor's appointment. Bill had his first stroke after we moved there, and it was difficult for him to get around and my back had gotten much worse. I have had a pinched sciatic nerve for years and am constantly in pain, some days better than others.

It was not working out for us in the condo, so in 2001 my daughter encouraged us to move to the Atlanta area where she lived. They always drove eight hours to get to us, and we needed to be closer to her. I sold the townhouse in Vilano Village and moved to an apartment in Duluth, Georgia about a mile and a half away from my daughter's home.

Bill and I lived in a lovely apartment in Duluth, for one year, near the front of the complex. We had a garage, but it was not attached to our apartment. This meant that we had a little walk to get to our apartment whenever we went to the store or out anywhere. This was OK for the first year, but then our mobility got a little more challenging the second year, so when our lease was up, we moved to another apartment toward the back of the same complex with an attached garage.

I have a sweet story to tell you. One day, shortly after we moved to the second apartment, there was a knock at our door. I went to the door and found a lovely young woman standing there. She introduced herself as Laurie and said, "Tomorrow, I am moving into an apartment in this row of apartments. My father and I came over today to move some shelving in the laundry room to get ready for the cable company installation tomorrow. He brought his tool box, but his hammer is not in his tool box. Do you have a hammer we could borrow for a little while?" I didn't know this person, but she seemed sincere and I somewhat sternly said, "Yes, I have a hammer you can borrow, but it is my father's hammer, and I want you to make sure I get it back." She did bring the hammer back the same day when they were finished with their work. We got into a conversation, and I told her that my daughter now lived in the apartment across the way, and it would be nice if they met each other. At the time, Laurie had a daughter in high school and a son in college.

They moved in that following weekend and on Monday, when her daughter, Rachael, came home from school, she had forgotten to take her key with her and was locked out of their apartment. Rachael came to our door and told us her situation and asked if she could come in to use the phone to call her mom at work. She came in, called her mom, and I asked her to stay with us until her mom came home from work. We had a delightful visit with this young girl.

I told my daughter about Laurie and her daughter and encouraged her to meet Laurie. My daughter was going to an outdoor concert that weekend with some other gals, and she called Laurie and invited her to go along. Laurie was concerned to leave her daughter alone, so I said, "We would be glad to have her for dinner and make sure she is OK, so you can go to the concert." My daughter told Laurie that she had never known me to let anyone borrow "Pappy's hammer." Somehow, I just knew that Laurie and her daughter where special.

Laurie and my daughter became fast friends. Laurie and Rachael have been very special friends to me and my daughter ever since. And to think, it all started with "Pappy's hammer."

After living in the apartment for two years, I saw that I was unable to take care of Bill, whose health was getting worse, and the pinched nerve in my back was getting to be more painful. Also, we were bored living in an apartment with very little socialization with folks our age. Most of the people living there were still of working age, and my daughter was still working. I decided that we needed a change and wanted to look for an independent living facility where we could be around folks our age and have people to play cards with and do other social activities. I was bored with nothing to do all day. When we visited Atlanta at other times over the years, my daughter and I would go look at different retirement homes to see what they were like, so I could make a decision on the right spot for me when the time came for me to make that decision.

CHAPTER 61

Delmar Gardens

AFTER MANY VISITS, we found a place called Delmar Gardens. We read and liked what we saw, and the next question was, "Do you have an active bridge group here?" They said they did, and that was the deciding factor that made up our minds that this was the place to go because Bill and I both enjoyed bridge and the stimulation it gave our brains. Bill and I moved there to a lovely two bedroom apartment in 2003, and I was still driving my 1999 Buick Park Avenue. I made wonderful friends there and enjoyed it very much.

We moved in and, since no one there played Rummikub, a game which we also enjoyed, we introduced this fun game. Bill and I would go down to the common area that was called "The Garden Room" and play the game.

After that, people seemed to be drawn to the game, so we taught the first new player, and it gained in popularity. Now, you can see as many as three tables of the game being played at one time. At first, we only had my game, and the activity director saw that more people wanted to play, so she bought us four more games. Many an hour was spent with the game and getting to know more of our lovely residents. I also started another group for bridge. We had two groups of bridge playing every week. We made many friends and had many good times.

I gave up driving in 2004 because it was too dangerous to drive in the Atlanta area. It made me very nervous, so I decided that it was not smart to take the risks of hurting someone else or me in an accident. We had a bus that took us everywhere we wanted to go. My daughter would come and take us places also. I stayed independent as long as I could safely do so.

Bill was a great companion. I would get a little upset with him sometimes but never anything major. He never got upset with me, and I know for sure that he loved me as I was. I was probably not the easiest person in the world to get along with. He did not seem to have his way; whatever was my way, was his way.

We golfed, traveled and entertained a lot over 19 years. Those were the best 19 years of my life living with a man. I often said to him, "You know, you have lasted a lot longer than my husbands." I also said, "You've been a lot nicer to me than my husbands, too." I don't know what it would've been like if we had married. I was used to having a place and everything must be in its place. Well, that does not make for a very good relationship with a husband or anybody else. I like to think that my way is the best way, knowing very well that is not always the best way.

In 2006, Bill went back to Pennsylvania for a visit. While he was there, his health continued to fail and his daughter was still working. Not wanting to leave him alone at home all day, she got him enrolled in an assisted living home near her home. She was able to see him every day on her way home from work. Unfortunately, he only lived for another three months, until he passed away. I did not think when he left that day on the first of June that it would be the last time that I would ever see him. I miss him every day, and he has been gone now for eight years. I called him every Saturday morning at 10 o'clock to talk to him. He said that he always sat there anxiously waiting for my calls. The last day that I talked to him before he died, for some reason, I said to him, "I love you." I never felt that it was necessary to say those words before. I always tried to show him all my love by sharing everything that I had and taking care of him during his many illnesses.

The children all loved him dearly. My daughters both told him that they wished that they would have had a dad like him. He was so good and kind to all of them. My family was glad that I had someone with me, and I am sure that Bill's family felt equally relieved to know that he had a companion to count on and enjoy life with, since his wife passed away. My grandchildren called him "Papa Bill."

We traveled and did many wonderful things. Bill was a gentle man, the likes of which I had never known. We began our companionship that was to last 19 years, until he passed away. What started out to be a two week vacation, turned out to be a 19 year close relationship. I miss him every day of my life. He was one of the many blessings in my life.

After Bill passed away, I moved within DelMar Gardens to a one bedroom apartment. Once again, I was downsizing. By this time, I had downsized four or five times since retirement.

I ate some meals in the dining room, but mostly, I fixed my own meals in my apartment that I could make in the crock-pot, microwave or toaster oven. Sometimes, I went to the dining room, just to be social and get out of my apartment. Sometimes, I just went down for tea and a chat with my girlfriends while they ate. We played Rummikub and hand-and-foot canasta. We also played bingo and Pokeno. And of course, I played bridge many times a week. I met many late-in-life friends there. I also took up growing African violets. I had the perfect spot for them in my apartment near my sliding glass doors. They were very happy plants and gave me hours of enjoyment.

I thought I would be there until the day my soul left this earth or my next adventure in this life.

I do not know how many more years I have or if I even have a year, but I'm ready when the good Lord is ready for me. God has been good to me and surely had his hand on my shoulder all of my life.

CHAPTER **62**

Going Back Home

IT WAS IN June of 2012, at 96 years of age, that I decided to make my last trip to Pennsylvania to see the island and friends.

On June 17th, my daughter and I loaded the car and started on our journey. We made it to Troutville, Virginia the first day. We checked into the hotel, freshened up a bit and started looking for a good place to have our dinner. We finally ended up at a restaurant that served good, old-fashioned meals. After eating, we returned to our room, relaxed for a while and then retired. Next morning, we got up, showered and again were on our way to Delaware where we would visit my grandson and his family. It was a lovely visit and a delicious dinner. We were "road" tired and went back to our hotel to bed. The next morning, we got up and spent most of the morning visiting with my grandson and family and then hit the road again. We headed for my son-in-law and his wife's home where we were spending the next week. They gave us their room for our convenience, and they slept in their guest room. The accommodations were delightful, and the food was superb. We would like to have had all of our meals there, but we had so many things planned with life-time friends that we were only home in the evenings.

Over the next week, we met with several of my employees that worked for me over the years, who helped me start my business. We saw Glen Condo, who worked for me when he was young, before he went in the Navy. He was so dependable and a wonderful young man. Of course, he is older now and has a thriving business of his own. It gave me great pleasure to see him doing so well.

After that, we went to see Ruth Yarrison and Teenie Courter, who were also wonderful people and very instrumental in getting the business started. Bill Corter and his lovely wife took us on a tour of many of the places of which we had fond memories. On Wednesday afternoon, after a delicious lunch, Margie and Rich took us to the Millbrook Playhouse to see a matinee. Thursday evening, Jerry and Sandy Blanchard took us to Ruby Tuesdays for dinner and then to the Millbrook Playhouse for another play. They brought one of my former employees and his wife with them to the restaurant, who I was delighted to see after all these years.

The next day, we went to visit a very dear friend, who was like a sister to me, and she also came and cleaned house for me every Thursday. These were special days for me. She always brought me a treat to have with my coffee at ten o'clock break. My house was always done to a tee, including my washing and ironing. I never did figure out how she did so much in one day, but I guess she had a system. Whenever we visit her these days, she always has a special treat for me to take home. It is several kinds of her good home-made jellies, whoopee-pies and applesauce. I eat of these sparingly so they will last as long as possible. Helen White will always have a special place in my heart.

I was told that another friend, who I always felt was like a son to me, had a stroke, but someone along the way said that he loved having visitors. We went to see him and his wife at their lovely farm. We talked for awhile and he seemed pleased that we had come to visit. He said to me that he never knew a woman who was as hard working and was such a good business woman. He was instrumental in helping me get my business back into operation again after the 1972 flood.

After the flood, he would often stop by and stick his head in the door of the plant and holler, "Louise, it is time for a coffee break."

We would go to the house where a pot of coffee was always brewing and have a cup of coffee and sometimes a cookie, talk about business and things that were happening in our lives. Then, he would be on his way, and I would go back to work. I will never forget the kindness he showed me, and he is in my prayers every night.

On this trip, we also asked the current owners of the old homestead if we could visit their home where I grew up. They were very gracious in allowing us to come in their home. They asked me questions about the original home before it had been remodeled by the previous owners. I was delighted to see that the integrity of the exterior of the home has been kept in excellent condition and the interior was delightful as well. They had us for tea and cookies after the tour, and the visit was very special to me.

After that, we went back to our host and hostess and spent the last two days visiting with them. The next day, we loaded up and started back to Georgia. Again, we went as far as Troutville, Virginia to spend the night and went the rest of the way the next day. We were very tired travelers and glad to be back home.

This was not to be my last trip to Pennsylvania. My daughter and I traveled there again in September 2013 and July 2014. We had enjoyable trips seeing friends and remembering our lives, way back then! There may be yet another trip back home in 2015, if I am able to do so.

Now, here I am at the age of 98 in the year of 2014, with one daughter, three grandchildren and seven great-grandchildren.

What more of this life could I ask?

Beautiful mountain home on Irish Lane where we stay with Margie and Rich Novosel when we visit Pennsylvania.

Me and Margie on a four-wheeler on Irish Lane.

CHAPTER 63

Dogwood Forest

IN 2012, I made the decision that after nine years at DelMar Gardens Independent Living Community, I needed a little more assistance with everyday living chores. Delmar Gardens had an assisted living wing, but I wanted to move closer to my daughter if I was going to switch to assisted living. My daughter and I started looking for an assisted living community that was even closer to her home than where I was currently residing. I decided on a lovely small community only six miles from my daughter's house called Dogwood Forest. I see my daughter almost every day, and she also volunteers as a gardener in our two lovely court yards at this community.

The assistance I receive from the staff at Dogwood Forest is very re-assuring, caring and encouraging. The hardest part of living a long life is giving up your independence as your body slows down. Daily chores become more difficult to perform without some assistance. As always, I still have that independent streak running through my veins, and I only ask for assistance when I know I really need it. I try not to let my pride rule my decisions where my safety or health is concerned. As Bette Davis is quoted as saying, "Getting Old Is Not For Sissies!" AMEN to that!!

Dogwood Forest staff L to R: Kelly, Lisa, Erik, Amy, and Jamie.

CHAPTER **64**

Growing Where I Was Planted

AFTER KILLING ONE or two chickens a week in my cellar in 1945 and taking them to my kitchen to eviscerate them, little did I know that I had started a career that was to last 35 years and ultimately make me a millionaire. It happened ten years later in my life than I had originally planned to retire, but better late than never.

I am one that always had to learn the hard way, but that did not seem to keep me from getting where I wanted to be — the dream of one day becoming a millionaire. I did not make it much past the million, but I made it. I made it enough to say that I was there. I have lived a wonderful life for the last 34 years in retirement because of my hard work and dedication toward my goal. I have made many good friends in life and many of them have passed away.

The way that I have survived is by taking the good out of every experience in life and letting the bad float away. My entire life, I have tried to "grow and bloom where I was planted." Over all these years of life, this philosophy has served me well.

Me and my daughter, Pat, taken in 2014.

CPSIA information can be obtained at www.ICGtesting.com
Printed in the USA
LVOW11s1014140515

438487LV00004B/177/P

9 781478 734536